DOUBLEDAY
New York
Toronto
London
Sydney
Auckland

Fresh from a Monastery Garden

BROTHER VICTOR-ANTOINE D'AVILA LATOURRETTE

PUBLISHED BY DOUBLEDAY
a division of Bantam Doubleday Dell Publishing Group, Inc.
1540 Broadway, New York, New York 10036

DOUBLEDAY and the portrayal of an anchor with a dolphin are trademarks of Doubleday,
a division of Bantam Doubleday Dell Publishing Group, Inc.

Book design by Donna Sinisgalli

Library of Congress Cataloging-in-Publication Data

D'Avila Latourrette, Victor-Antoine.
Fresh from a monastery garden / Brother Victor-Antoine d'Avila-Latourrette.
p.   cm.
I. Cookery (Vegetables)   I. Title.
TX801.D26   1998
641.6′5–dc2I   98-10356
CIP

ISBN 0-385-49039-9
Printed in the United States of America
November 1998
First Edition

1 3 5 7 9 10 8 6 4 2

To Elise Boulding,

who inspired me to write my first cookbook

To Margaret and Michael O'Keefe,

Carole Ann and Douglas Mercer, and to Barbara Etherington,

faithful and always most cherished friends

CONTENTS

An Easy Way to Find
Your Favorite Vegetable Recipes

Fresh from a Monastery Garden brings to the kitchens of its readers not only nearly two hundred inventive ways to enhance vegetables as they are prepared for meals, but also serves as a convenient guide to the essential background of vegetables themselves. Accordingly, unlike my previous books, which were organized seasonally, this book follows an entirely new plan. Each of the vegetables in common use in North America is the focus of an independent section, with its own brief introduction emphasizing individuality, origin, and traditional uses in cooking. It will be surprising to see how these have changed over the years! Vegetables once considered exotic are now as common as tomatoes. These brief descriptions will be especially helpful to those interested in trying some of the vegetables that aren't usually found every day in meals prepared in our homes and elsewhere.

Each vegetable section will be found in alphabetical order, for convenience. (In the course of preparing this book, we have sometimes nicknamed it "the ABCs book," and you are encouraged to do the same.) Throughout the head notes and the recipes you will find suggestions for seasonal use, so the emphasis on freshness is also very much evident. At the end of the book, as an additional aid, you will find a seasonal organization of the vegetables covered in it.

It is important not to forget, however, that the seasons overlap, as do the use and availability of some vegetables, especially those harvested at the tail end of their season. For example, asparagus and peas are considered essentially spring vegetables; however, sometimes one continues to harvest and enjoy them throughout early summer. The same can be said of some summer vegetables like corn and tomatoes; their harvest and availability continue throughout the fall months until the hard frost kills the plants.

"This is what the Lord Almighty, the God of Israel, says . . .

plant gardens and eat what they produce."

JEREMIAH 39:5

"All sorts of grain which our own land doth yield

Was hither brought, and sown in every field:

As wheat and rye, barley, oats, bean and peas

Here all thrive and they profit from them raise,

All sorts of roots and herbs in gardens grow—

Parsnips, carrots, turnips or what you'll sow,

Onions, melons, cucumbers, radishes,

Skirets, beets, coleworts and fair cabbages.

WILLIAM BRADFORD,
Governor of Plymouth County, 1621

INTRODUCTION

A few years ago, a fine young student who occasionally liked to visit our small monastery went off to France. While there, he decided to see some of the many monasteries that are to be encountered everywhere across the French landscape. Upon his return to this country, I asked him what he had discovered or what had most impressed him in the places he had visited.

Without hesitation, the young man exclaimed, "Ah, the gardens of the monasteries, those gardens lovingly tended by the monks."

At first, I was surprised at his response. I had expected him to mention perhaps the beauty of the monastic churches or the unforgettable music of the chants in the Offices, for example. Of course, he found the prayerful Offices to be a deeply spiritual experience, he said, but he was most enchanted by what he found in the monastic gardens. "There is real life in those gardens," he went on, "and one can almost feel the pulse of a particular monastic community by the work that is being accomplished there in the gardens." And he recalled for me how the charming and brightly colored miniatures from the ancient monastic manuscripts, where we often see the monk or the nun depicted steadily at work in the garden, suddenly became alive for him and deeply expressive of meaning.

In all our monasteries, of course, the occupation of gardening is as old as monastic life itself. Gardens and the constant tending of them have always been an integral part of our tradition. The first monks went about elaborating the principles of monastic gardening in the deserts of Egypt and Palestine, in the same way and at the same time that they elaborated the first rules and principles that were to become the base of their monastic living. For example, we read in an early life of Saint Antony, the first monk and the father of all monks, an episode that relates to his work in the garden: "These vines and these little trees did he plant; the pool did he contrive, with much labor for the watering of his garden; with his rake did he break up the earth for many years."

It is obvious from this description that Saint Antony worked very hard in his garden, and that the main reason for cultivating it was to provide food for himself and other monks, as well as for the poor and the pilgrims that came to see him. Saint Antony took to heart the biblical counsel that one must eat from the labor of one's hands. Two centuries later, Saint Benedict would insist on the importance of the same teaching by stating in his Rule that "they are truly monks when they live by the labor of their hands, as did our fathers and the Apostles." That meant for Saint Benedict that the monks had to work long hours in their gardens, orchards, and mills, producing the food necessary for the monastic table. And since the monastic regimen tends to be almost exclusively vegetarian, the cultivation of vegetable gardens and the care and maintenance of vineyards and orchards became of primary importance in the life of all monasteries. In this context, we can understand how some monks became passionate gardeners down through the centuries. There is, for example, the eighth-century monk Walafrid Strabo of the Abbey of Reichenau, who went so far as to praise gardening in a work called *De cultura hortorum* (On the Cultivation of Gardens).

And it was not only the monks who devoted time and skills in great measure to the work and the art of gardening. The nuns, living under the same Rule of Saint Benedict, invested their unique talents in this work, as we see from the case of the twelfth-century abbess Saint Hildegard of Bingen. Her combined knowledge of agriculture and medicine inspired her to write two treatises on the nutritional and medicinal qualities of the various plants, herbs, and vegetables that her nuns cultivated in the monastery gardens. Saint Hildegard recommended strongly that the vegetables prepared in the kitchen be fresh and recently harvested in order to retain the vital energies of the produce and all nutritional benefits. Saint Hildegard insisted on the principle that as human beings we don't exist in isolation but always live in a mutually dependent relationship with the whole universe. Thus it was extremely important to her that people should learn to live harmoniously with the rhythm of the seasons, and this was to include a diet based on the fresh vegetables and fruits harvested from their gardens and orchards. She firmly believed in what we would today call an "organic-biological process" that respects the rhythm of the seasons, the inner cohesion of all creation, and the natural laws that help maintain order and balance in the universe. By living thus, Saint Hildegard believed, human beings could achieve balance and health in their own personal lives.

History has shown that both monks and nuns have always been vigilant stewards and avid cultivators of the land entrusted to them. The time allotted to them each year for full- or part-time gardening, from the moment of planting the first seed to the moment the last vegetable is harvested, is for the monk or nun gardener a rewarding and, indeed, an intense time of joy. This is so in spite of the hard and never-ending nature of the work. Of course, the real reward is felt when the fresh new vegetables begin to be served at the monastic table, delighting all who partake. Gardening in a monastery is both a task and an art. It is the solid experience accumulated over many years that brings the monk gardener mastery of the proper methods and many intricate secrets necessary to achieve reliable success. Nothing, indeed, can supplant that experience! The monk or nun gardener, just as anyone else who is serious about this, needs to be sensitively attuned to the growing seasons, to the local weather, to the quality of the soil, and so forth . . . and always to allow Mother Nature to be the guide.

Each season has its own significance. There is a time to prepare and build the soil, a time for planting and germination, a time for cultivation and growth, and a time for yielding fruit and harvesting. Each season, too, provides its own unique variety in vegetables—some for spring and summer, some for fall and even winter. Living and gardening in tune with the seasons permit the monk or nun gardener to provide for the table vegetables rich with vitamins and nutrients, wonderful with the taste of freshness, and beautiful in exquisite colors and textures. The vegetables thus harvested are brought to the monastery kitchen, where they are treated with great respect. It remains for the cook to use talent and taste to create imaginative dishes that can be savored and remembered by the monastic palate long after the food has been consumed.

Of course, not everyone has a plot of land or the time to cultivate a garden, infinitely desirable as this may be. However, in the present day and age, that is not a good reason for passing up fresh vegetables. Today we have enviably wide opportunities to find fresh vegetables at supermarkets throughout the land, as well as at farmers' markets, at roadside stands, and in a variety of other ways in cities and in the country. And freshness makes all the difference in the world. Any cook concerned about solid nutrition and wonderful flavors will seek out the freshest possible vegetables to be found locally. Fresh vegetables retain most of their original nutritional value and provide a standard of texture and taste that is excellence itself.

The recipes in this book do not include meat. This does not mean that they are designed for the vegetarian alone. Vegetables are for everyone! In creating and presenting these new recipes to the public, it never entered my mind that they were to be used by only one group of people. On the contrary, these recipes were created, first, for each and every person who is interested in a healthy diet; and second, for all those who are tired of presenting vegetables at the table in the same old way and are looking for good, innovative recipes that reflect the boundless opportunities that vegetables present. While many of these recipes are self-sufficient as they are, the majority of them also go well with meat, egg, or fish dishes. Some may be used to create wonderful soups or appetizers; others, for salads; and others, either as the main dish or as accompaniment to another main course. It will be up to the imagination of the chef to adapt or re-create these recipes as a surprise for family, friends, or guests. My most ardent hope is that vegetables will be rediscovered in a new light, be in demand more than ever before, and, most of all, become the essential foundation of a cuisine that will be both healthier and more refined.

Finally, I wish to use this Introduction as an opportunity to thank all those dear friends here in the United States and in France who encouraged me and supported me during the long, sometimes burdensome, but always rewarding task of preparing this book. First of all, I wish to thank Trace Murphy, my editor at Doubleday; Andrew Corbin, also of Doubleday, for his support and technical assistance; and Howard Sandum, my literary agent, for requesting this book and believing in the vision that it became. I wish to thank also all those who helped type the manuscript: Sister Joan Regis Catherwood, RSHM, who typed the largest portion of it, but also Sister Ana M. Martinez of Transfiguration Monastery, Windsor, New York; Paschal Meier; and Jennifer Wyman, secretary to our friend John Conrad—all of whom lent their helping hands through to the end so as to complete the manuscript in time for our deadline. Heartfelt thanks also to Mark Adams for providing me with the quote from the beautiful poem by William Bradford.

I hope these recipes help enhance *la bonne table* in your home, and bring joy to you, your family, and your friends.

br. Victor-Antoine, monk
February 10, 1998
Feast of Saint Scholastica, abbess
sister of our father Saint Benedict

Fresh from a
Monastery Garden

Asparagus

(asparagus officinalis)

Asparagus was well known in antiquity; we find it, for example, carved in the ancient Egyptian hieroglyphics. We know also that the Greeks used it as an aphrodisiac and the Romans enriched a form of what we now call pasta by adding creamed asparagus to the flour, thus enhancing both the texture and the taste of the pasta.

However, for a long time afterward, asparagus was neglected in general cooking until it reappeared or was reintroduced in European kitchens around the time of the eighteenth century. From there it traveled to America, where it has been widely cultivated and greatly appreciated at the table ever since. At the beginning of spring we all feel exhilarated to see it arrive in large quantities in our local markets and roadside produce stands. When choosing fresh asparagus, in the market we would do well to select stalks that are firm with no trace of dryness or aging.

There are several varieties of asparagus. In Europe, the white asparagus is particularly cherished at the table. In North America, however, that variety is less widely known; here, it is the green asparagus that is more typically served and savored. Asparagus stalks, like corn, taste better when they are eaten soon after they are picked; therefore they should not be kept for a long time in the refrigerator, but should be consumed while as fresh as possible.

As with other vegetables, asparagus can be prepared in a variety of forms—creamed into a soup, for example, or served as whole stalks, either hot or chilled or at room temperature. Usually asparagus is best when served alone or separately from other dishes, so that its unique flavor can be appreciated. This train of thought often leads asparagus to be served in the form of a soup or appetizer, as in some of the recipes presented here.

Asparagus

Asparagus Milanese
(Asperges à la Milanaise)

4 SERVINGS

1 pound fresh asparagus

salt to taste

2 tablespoons lemon juice

$^1/_2$ cup grated Parmesan cheese

butter

4 eggs

freshly ground pepper to taste

1. Gather the asparagus stalks into a bunch and tie them with a string. Place them in a good-size casserole filled with boiling water, add the salt and lemon juice, and blanch them for about 4 or 5 minutes until they become tender though remaining firm. Drain them well.

2. Butter thoroughly a long, flat ovenproof dish and place the drained asparagus stalks carefully in it. Cover them with the Parmesan cheese and place them in a warm oven (300°) for about 10 minutes.

3. Just before serving, melt the butter in a large skillet or frying pan, break the eggs into it and cook the whites well while retaining the freshness of the yolk. Sprinkle with salt and pepper to taste.

4. Serve the asparagus on hot plates, carefully placing one cooked egg on top of each serving. Serve immediately.

Note: This is a perfect dish for a Sunday or festive brunch, and it can also be served as the main dish, accompanied by plenty of fresh Italian bread, for a light supper in the springtime, when asparagus is in abundance.

Fresh from a
Monastery Garden

Asparagus Risotto

5 tablespoons butter or olive oil

1 medium-size onion, chopped

1 celery stalk, thinly sliced

1 cup cut-up asparagus, sliced 1 inch long

2 cups Arborio rice or other rice of your preference

5 cups boiling water or vegetable broth

1 bouillon cube (of your own flavor)

1 cup dry white wine

salt and freshly ground black pepper to taste

$^{1}/_{2}$ teaspoon thyme

$^{1}/_{2}$ cup grated Parmesan or Romano cheese

additional grated cheese for the table

1. Melt the butter in a heavy, good-sized saucepan. Add the onion, celery, and asparagus. Sauté them lightly for about 3 minutes or until they begin to wilt. Add more butter or oil if necessary.

2. Add the rice and stir constantly for about 1 to 2 minutes until it becomes well coated and begins to change color slightly. Add the boiling water gradually while stirring continually. Add the bouillon cube and wine and continue stirring. Midway into the cooking, add the salt, pepper, and thyme and continue stirring until the rice is cooked.

3. When the rice is cooked, add the grated cheese and stir vigorously until it is all absorbed and incorporated into the rice. Serve the risotto hot and place additional grated cheese on the table.

Note: This delicious risotto makes a wonderful main course when entertaining family or friends.

Asparagus

Asparagus Puree

1 pound asparagus

2 teaspoons lemon juice

2 shallots, chopped and minced

6 tablespoons dry white wine

1 8-ounce container crème fraîche
  or sour cream

salt and pepper to taste

3 teaspoons tarragon, finely chopped

1. Trim the asparagus, peeling the hard parts and removing the stalks. Place the asparagus in a large saucepan with salted water and bring to a boil. Add the lemon juice and blanch the asparagus for 6 to 8 minutes until they become tender. Drain them well.

2. Put the cooked asparagus in a food processor and puree them thoroughly.

3. Place the shallots and white wine in a casserole and heat lightly; after a minute add the crème fraîche or the sour cream. Stir continually until the cream begins to bubble. At this point, add the pureed asparagus, salt, pepper, and chopped tarragon, and continue stirring until all the ingredients are well mixed. Serve hot. If you want to make this in advance, butter an ovenproof dish and put the puree in it. Place in a preheated oven to keep the puree hot until you are ready to serve.

Note: This is an excellent accompaniment for egg, fish, or meat dishes.

Fresh from a
Monastery Garden

Asparagus Batonnets

20 asparagus (5 per person), trimmed

8 tablespoons flour (approximately)

2 eggs, beaten

bread crumbs

oil (for frying)

1. Cut the asparagus into pieces 6 to 7 inches long. (Discard the bottom part.) Place the asparagus in salted boiling water and cook them for about 5–6 minutes. Drain the asparagus, rinse them in cold water, and dry them with paper towels.

2. With great care, roll each asparagus first in the flour, then in the eggs, and then in the bread crumbs.

3. Pour the frying oil into a skillet and when it is hot, place the asparagus, four at a time, in it and cook them carefully, watching that they are fried on all sides and at the same time remain intact.

4. When all the asparagus are done, if they are to be served later, place them in an elongated, well-buttered ovenproof dish and keep hot in a 200° preheated oven for about 10–15 minutes until you are ready to serve.

Note: Serve the batonnets as an appetizer or as an accompaniment to the main course.

7

Asparagus

Saint Michael Asparagus Soup

½ pound asparagus, tough ends removed,
   cut into 1-inch lengths

1 potato, peeled and diced

4 shallots, sliced

2 medium carrots, sliced

2 quarts water

1 cup half and half

2 tablespoons butter or margarine

salt and pepper to taste

1. Cook the vegetables in boiling salted water until they are tender. Put the soup in a blender and whirl it to create a smooth mixture.

2. Return the soup to the pot, add the half and half, butter, salt, and pepper, and bring the soup to a boil while stirring. Cover the pot and let the soup simmer for another 10 minutes. Serve hot.

Fresh from a
Monastery Garden

Asparagus Salad Mimosa

4 SERVINGS

20 fresh asparagus, trimmed

1 small head of Boston lettuce

2 cups cut-up cooked beets, sliced julienne style

4 hard-boiled eggs, chopped

VINAIGRETTE

8 tablespoons olive oil

4 tablespoons cider vinegar

1 teaspoon French mustard

1 shallot, finely chopped and minced

salt and pepper to taste

1. Bring 2 quarts of water to a boil in a large saucepan. Add a pinch of salt and the trimmed asparagus and cook for about 3 minutes. Drain and rinse them under cold water. Drain them again and set aside.

2. Wash, rinse, and dry the lettuce leaves well. Set them aside.

3. Prepare the vinaigrette by mixing together all the ingredients.

4. On each of the four salad plates, arrange 3 leaves of lettuce. Place 5 asparagus on top and the julienned beets on both sides of the asparagus. Distribute the chopped hard-boiled eggs evenly over each serving as garnish. Just before serving, pour some of the vinaigrette on each dish and serve immediately.

Asparagus

Artichokes

(cynara scolymus)

*L*ike many other vegetable species that have survived to our day, the artichoke had its origins in the countries surrounding the Mediterranean Sea. In ancient Greek literature, there are frequent references to the artichoke. The Egyptians, besides eating them, also consumed the boiled salted water in which they were cooked as a medicine for certain types of ailments. The Romans often used the artichoke as an accompaniment to their most gourmet dishes, frequently serving it with their finest fish dishes. It was through the Romans that the artichoke was introduced into Spain and France and later to other areas of Europe. A bit forgotten by the aristocracy during the Middle Ages, the artichoke was rediscovered and revived during the Renaissance, first by a certain Filippo Strozzi in Florence around 1466, and later in France by Catherine de' Médicis for whom the artichoke was a favorite vegetable—indeed she considered it a delicacy. During her reign, she expanded its cultivation throughout France. By the time of King Henry IV, not only was the artichoke eaten routinely in the cities and countryside of France but it was also used as an aphrodisiac. From France, Spain, and Italy, the cultivation of the artichoke expanded, especially early in this century, to other countries with milder climates such as Argentina and to certain areas of the United States, especially California.

The artichoke today is an integral part of certain kinds of refined cuisine, especially those that come to us from France, Spain, Italy, Greece, etc. It is often used in salads served as an appetizer, or as one of the main ingredients in dishes such as risotto and pasta. The artichoke contains vitamins A, B, and C, which make it a desirable vegetable from a health point of view.

It takes a certain amount of practice and patience to cook artichokes, which is why when pressed for time, the reluctant cook should not hesitate to use frozen or even canned artichokes in ordinary or everyday cooking.

13

Artichokes

Artichokes Basque Style

(ARTICHAUTS À LA BASQUAISE)

4 SERVINGS

4 artichokes, trimmed

4 tablespoons lemon juice

1 small head of leaf lettuce

4 medium-size tomatoes, sliced in
   quarters lengthwise

4 hard-boiled eggs, sliced in rounds

1 small red onion, thinly sliced

green olives

VINAIGRETTE

7 tablespoons virgin olive oil

2 tablespoons wine vinegar

2 tablespoons lemon juice

salt and freshly ground pepper to taste

1. Cook the artichokes in salted water mixed with the 4 tablespoons of lemon juice for 30 minutes until the artichokes become tender. Remove them from the heat and rinse them in cold water. Separate and discard the leaves, remove the artichoke hearts, and chill them until ready to use.

2. Just before you are ready to serve, arrange the whole lettuce leaves in four separate salad plates. Place 1 artichoke heart in the center of the lettuce leaves. Surround each artichoke heart with tomato slices alternating with hard-boiled egg slices. Add the thin onion slices and some olives around each artichoke.

3. Prepare the vinaigrette, mix it well, and pour some over each salad.

Note: This dish makes a wonderful appetizer any time of the year.

Fresh from a
Monastery Garden

Artichokes Greek Style
(ARTICHAUTS À LA GRECQUE)

4 SERVINGS

4 tablespoons lemon juice

16 small artichokes

8 tablespoons olive oil

1 bay leaf

finely chopped fresh cilantro (a few sprigs)

salt and pepper to taste

2 ripe tomatoes, peeled, seeded, and sliced
   into small pieces

1. To prepare the artichokes for cooking, break off the leaves at the bottom and place the artichoke on a board sideways. Using a sharp knife, cut the lower leaves off up to where the heart of the artichoke is found. Then proceed to trim and cut off the leaves above the heart of the artichoke. Cut off and trim the rest of the leaves following the same procedure, being careful to see that the artichoke hearts remain intact. As you finish trimming each artichoke, place the hearts in a casserole filled with cold water and 4 tablespoons of lemon juice and leave them for $^1/_2$ hour.

2. To cook the artichokes, make use of a good-size frying pan with considerable depth. Place the artichokes in the pan. Add 6 tablespoons of the olive oil, bay leaf, finely chopped cilantro, salt, and pepper, and cover up to the top of the artichokes with the lemon water. Cover the pan and cook the artichokes for about 15 minutes over medium-low heat until they are tender. Allow the artichokes to cool in the frying pan with the remaining liquid.

3. Just before serving, drain the artichoke hearts with great care and place them in a good-size bowl. Add the tomatoes, a few extra drops of lemon juice, and 2 tablespoons of olive oil. Mix well and serve.

Note: This dish can be used as an appetizer, or as an accompaniment to the main course, or as a salad after the main course.

Artichokes

Artichoke Ragout
(RAGOÛT D'ARTICHAUTS)

4—6 SERVINGS

10 artichokes (or substitute 4 6-ounce cans artichokes in oil, well drained and rinsed in cold water)

4 tablespoons lemon juice

1 pound mushrooms

1 ounce butter

2 shallots, finely chopped and minced

4 sprigs chervil, finely chopped

lemon juice, as needed (concentrate may be used)

2 teaspoons flour or cornstarch

salt and pepper to taste

1. To get the artichokes ready for cooking, break off all the leaves at the bottom and place the vegetable on a board sideways. Using a sharp knife, cut the lower leaves off up to where the heart of the artichoke is found. Then proceed to trim and cut off the leaves above the heart of the artichoke. Following the same procedure, cut off and trim the rest of the leaves, watching carefully that the artichoke hearts remain intact. As each artichoke gets trimmed, place the heart in a casserole filled with cold water to which one must add 4 tablespoons of lemon juice. Leave the artichokes in the lemony water for 1/2 hour.

2. Boil the artichokes for 12 minutes. (If you substitute canned artichokes, boil them only for 1 minute.) Drain and set them aside. Remove the excess or remaining hairy parts, and slice them evenly.

3. Clean and trim the mushrooms, leaving them whole and cutting off only the stem parts.

4. Melt the butter in a deep skillet or frying pan. Add the artichoke hearts and mushrooms and sauté them lightly for 4–5 minutes.

5. After 5 minutes, add the chopped shallots and chervil, 2 teaspoons of flour or cornstarch, salt, and pepper, and mix all the ingredients thoroughly. Stir often. After a minute or two, cover the skillet and turn off the heat. Serve the ragout warm.

Note: This ragout makes an excellent appetizer any time of the year.

Fresh from a
Monastery Garden

Artichoke Salad

12 artichokes (or substitute 3 6-ounce
    cans artichokes in oil, well drained and
    rinsed in cold water)
4 hard-boiled eggs, sliced in quarters
4 tomatoes, sliced in quarters

12 black olives, pitted
I small red onion, sliced in rings
finely chopped fresh basil as garnish

VINAIGRETTE

7 tablespoons olive oil
3 tablespoons balsamic vinegar

salt and freshly ground pepper to taste

1. If you are using fresh artichokes, prepare them as directed in the previous recipe (page 16). If you are using canned artichokes, boil them for only 1 minute.

2. In four serving dishes, distribute evenly the artichokes, eggs, tomatoes, and black olives. Spread the onion rings on top.

3. Just before serving, prepare the vinaigrette by mixing all the ingredients well. Pour evenly over each dish, garnish the top with the chopped basil, and serve.

Note: This dish can be used either as a regular salad or as an appetizer or as a main dish for lunch.

Artichokes

Avocados

(persea americana)

The avocado, contrary to popular belief, is not a vegetable but a fruit. The confusion stems from the frequent culinary use of the avocado as a vegetable, and not as a fruit. Like most vegetables, the avocado is primarily served at the table in salty dishes and is seldom used or served in a sweet fashion as a dessert, at least not in the United States. However, in the kitchen, avocado use may vary to include its proper role as a fruit in a sweet form. Suffice to say that here in this collection I resort to common local use, and I treat it exclusively as a vegetable.

The avocado tree has been cultivated for centuries in the Caribbean Islands and in Central and South America. In the twentieth century, its cultivation has extended to other areas of the world such as Israel, Turkey, South Africa, Australia, and here in the United States where the climate warrants its growth, such as in Florida and California. Obviously, as the market demand for the avocado increases, its cultivation for commercial use continues to extend to other parts of the world as well.

The original Aztec name for the avocado is *ahuacatt*, and from there it was transformed into the Spanish *aguacate*, and the English *avocado*. The avocado fruit is oval or round in form, depending on its variety. Its inside flesh is usually yellow or pale green in color, developed around a large simple seed. Among the many varieties of avocado fruit, there are three that are more well known than the others. They differ according to their place of origin: Mexico, Central America (mostly Guatemala), and the Caribbean Islands.

The avocado fruit contains a high degree of fat (sometimes as much as 25 percent oil). The avocado is rich in vitamin A and protein, riboflavin, and thiamine. It is obvious that the avocado has gained great popularity among vegetarians, who benefit immensely from using the avocado to balance their diet.

Because avocados in general don't have a long life expectancy and tend to ripen and discolor rather quickly, it is important that they be served as soon as possible after they are peeled and sliced. One way to preserve them and prolong their appearance is to mix them well with lemon juice. The lemon juice not only acts as a preservative but also enhances the avocado's original nutty flavor and makes it more distinct.

Avocados

Avocado and Tofu Dip

SEVERAL SERVINGS

2 ripe avocados, peeled

¹/₂ pound tofu

1 tablespoon paprika

2 tablespoons lemon juice

2 tablespoons olive oil

2 shallots or 1 small onion, chopped and
minced

4 tablespoons fresh cilantro, chopped and
minced

salt and pepper to taste

Mix all these ingredients in a food processor and whirl it for a few seconds. Check the seasonings and place the mixture in a bowl. Refrigerate it until you are ready to serve.

Note: It can be served with Mexican corn tortillas or with melba toast or ordinary crackers. It is a healthy and nutritious dip.

Fresh from a
Monastery Garden

Saints Peter and Paul Avocado Soup

4—6 SERVINGS

3 leeks, white parts only, trimmed and
    sliced

6 cups water

3 avocados, peeled and sliced in half

3 tablespoons lemon juice

1 8-ounce container low-fat sour cream

1 teaspoon paprika

salt and pepper to taste

lemon rind as garnish

1. Place the leeks in a casserole, add the water, and bring it to a boil. Lower the heat to medium-low and cook the leeks for about 15–20 minutes. Remove the casserole from the heat, allow the soup to cool, and then whirl it in a blender or food processor. Pour the mixture back into the casserole or into a large bowl.

2. Place the avocados, lemon juice, sour cream, paprika, and salt and pepper in the blender or food processor and whirl it for about 1 minute. Add this mixture to the leek mixture and blend all the ingredients well by hand. Place the soup in the refrigerator for at least 2 hours before serving. Serve it cold and add some lemon rind on the top of each serving as garnish.

This soup is often served in our monastery during the summer months, especially on June 29, the feast of the great apostles Peter and Paul, foundation stones of the Church of God, and whose icons are reverently venerated in our chapel.

Avocados

Avocado and Mâche Salad

4 small avocados, peeled and sliced
   lengthwise
I large bunch of mâche leaves, washed
   and dried

I cup fresh or frozen peas (large size)
I shallot, diced and minced
4 small cucumbers (cornichons), sliced

VINAIGRETTE

5 tablespoons hazelnut oil
3 tablespoons lemon juice

a pinch of paprika
salt and freshly ground pepper to taste

1. Place the vegetables in a large salad bowl.

2. Prepare the vinaigrette by mixing all the ingredients well. When ready to serve, pour the vinaigrette over the vegetables in the bowl and gently toss a few times until they are well coated. Serve immediately.

Note: This salad is usually best used as an appetizer for lunch or brunch. It is particularly attractive when you harvest the fresh mâche and peas from your garden.

Fresh from a
Monastery Garden

Avocado Salad with Goat Cheese

1 small head of Bibb lettuce, washed and drained

1 8-ounce long-sized (or elongated like a stick of butter) goat cheese, cut into 4 slices

2 avocados, peeled and sliced in half lengthwise

finely chopped fresh cilantro and chives as garnish

VINAIGRETTE

6 tablespoons olive oil

3 tablespoons lemon juice

salt and pepper to taste

1. Separate the lettuce leaves and arrange them on four individual salad dishes.

2. Place the 4 slices of goat cheese in a 350° oven under the broiler for 5 minutes until it begins to melt.

3. While the cheese is in the oven, place an avocado half on top of the lettuce on each dish.

4. Prepare the vinaigrette by mixing all the ingredients well. When the cheese is done place a slice on each avocado half. Pour some of the vinaigrette over each serving and sprinkle some finely chopped cilantro and chives on top as garnish.

Note: This is a delightful and nutritious appetizer all year round.

Avocados

Guacamole

4 ripe avocados, peeled and mashed

2 tomatoes, peeled, seeded, and chopped

1 medium-size onion, diced

1 small red pepper, diced

1 small green bell pepper, diced

3 tablespoons finely chopped fresh
   cilantro

2 tablespoons sour cream (or plain
   yogurt)

2 tablespoons lemon juice

salt and freshly ground pepper to taste

1. Place the mashed avocados in a deep bowl. Add the chopped tomatoes, diced onion, diced peppers, and finely chopped cilantro. Mix the ingredients well.

2. Add the sour cream, lemon juice, and salt and pepper to taste. Mix all the ingredients again very well, and then place the bowl in the refrigerator until serving time.

Fresh from a
Monastery Garden

Beans

(phaseolus vulgaris)

Beans have a long history, dating back to the ancient Greeks and Romans. However, it is well known that the popular common garden bean, or haricot as it is called in France, had its origin on the American continent. With the arrival of Christopher Columbus in the Americas, the first Europeans who accompanied him discovered the bean, first in Cuba and later in other parts of Central and South America, as well as in areas of North America, in what is known today as Arizona and Utah. From these American sources, beans made their way to Europe. In France, the first mention of beans is in a document dated around 1564, which relates that beans were cultivated in the region surrounding the town of Vienne, having been introduced from a monastery near Lisbon, Portugal. In Italy, we find mention of the first traces of bean cultivation around 1528 in the town of Belluno, where a certain Italian humanist named Valeriano started sowing beans imported from Peru. Valeriano considered the discovery of beans similar to the discovery of a treasure, and under his influence bean agriculture was extended to other regions of Italy. By the end of the sixteenth century, the cultivation and lore of beans was well established throughout Italy, France, and Spain. These regions were the basis for the further expansion of beans to other areas of the world.

Today, a great many varieties of beans are cultivated by serious gardeners all around the globe. Beans have become an integral part of the daily diet because they are rich in vitamin C, potassium, and calcium. Furthermore, beans are an excellent source of protein; they provide an essential substitute for meat in many vegetarian diets. Beans are sometimes divided into two categories: fresh or green beans harvested from the garden and eaten in their entirety (the pod along with the beans), and dried beans, which are harvested at the end of the season, then snapped from their shells, left out to dry, and preserved for future use in dry sealed containers. The following recipes incorporate various types of beans in either of these two forms. Among the principal types are the fresh green and yellow wax bean, the haricot vert, lima bean, the romano pole bean, all of which are cultivated yearly in our garden. Among the dried beans used frequently at the monastic table and therefore represented in this collection of recipes are fava beans, white navy beans, black beans, and lentils.

Beans

Green Bean Salad

(SALADE DE HARICOTS VERTS)

6 SERVINGS

1½ pounds French green beans
(or regular string beans)
½ pound fresh mushrooms
2 shallots

1 lemon
1 8-ounce container low-fat yogurt
salt and freshly ground pepper to taste

1. Trim the green beans and place them in a saucepan or casserole filled with cold water for 10 minutes.

2. Place the pan on the stove and bring the water to a boil. Lower the heat to medium-low and cook for 10 minutes. Drain the beans and rinse them in cold water. Set them aside.

3. Wash and clean the mushrooms well. Slice them thinly. Chop and mince the shallots.

4. Squeeze the juice of the lemon into a bowl, add the yogurt, salt, and pepper, and whisk thoroughly by hand or with the help of a mixer until the mixture turns into a smooth dressing.

5. When you are ready to serve, add the beans, mushrooms, and shallots to the bowl of dressing. Mix well and serve.

Note: This dish can be served as an appetizer or as a salad after the main course.

Fresh from a
Monastery Garden

Wax Bean Puree

6 SERVINGS

2 pounds wax beans, trimmed and broken in half (preferably use new tender beans)

1 shallot, chopped and minced

1 8-ounce container crème fraîche or light cream

6 tablespoons butter

salt and pepper to taste

finely chopped parsley as garnish

1. Cook the beans in a large saucepan in salted boiling water for 10–12 minutes. Drain the beans and rinse them in cold water. Puree the beans in a food processor until they turn into a smooth cream. Add the shallot and process the cream a bit more.

2. Heat the crème fraîche in a casserole and allow it to reduce a bit over low heat.

3. Melt the butter in a deep frying pan. After a minute or two, add the bean puree. Stir and slowly add the reduced crème fraîche, salt, and pepper. Mix well and cover the frying pan for a minute or two. Sprinkle on top of each serving some finely chopped parsley as garnish. Serve hot.

Note: The puree makes a wonderful accompaniment to a fish or meat dish.

Beans

Green Beans Portuguese Style

1 pound green string beans

a pinch of salt

4 tablespoons olive oil or lard

4 good-size tomatoes, peeled and cubed

salt and pepper to taste

chopped parsley as garnish

1. Trim the beans and place them in a casserole filled with cold water for 15 minutes. After that, place the casserole on the stove and bring the water to a boil. Add a pinch of salt, lower the heat to medium-low, cover the casserole, and cook the beans for about 10 minutes. They must remain firm and not be overcooked. Drain the beans and rinse them in cold water. Set them aside.

2. Pour the olive oil into a large, deep skillet, add the cubed tomatoes and salt and pepper to taste. Sauté the tomatoes briefly until they turn into a light sauce. (They must not be overcooked.) At this point, add the green beans and mix well with the tomato sauce until the beans are hot again. (A minute or two.) Serve the beans hot and sprinkle over them the finely chopped parsley as garnish.

Note: This recipe can also be used with wax beans, if you prefer them to green beans.

Fresh from a
Monastery Garden

Spicy Black Beans

1 pound black beans (dried or canned)

1/3 cup vegetable oil

3 onions, sliced

8 good-size tomatoes, peeled and chopped

4 garlic cloves, minced

2 celery stalks, finely sliced

1 jalapeño pepper, seeded and sliced

2 green bell peppers, seeded and sliced

1/3 cup chopped fresh cilantro

1/3 cup finely chopped fresh parsley

1 teaspoon cumin

1 teaspoon chili powder

salt and pepper to taste

1. Soak the dried beans overnight. Rinse them in cold water. Cook them in salted boiling water for 45 minutes. Discard the water. Put fresh water in the saucepan and boil again for about 20 minutes. Drain the beans and discard the water. This process can be avoided by using an equal amount of canned beans. If you use canned beans, they need to be rinsed in cold water and drained properly. Set the beans aside.

2. Heat the oil in a saucepan and add the onions, tomatoes, garlic, celery, peppers, cilantro, and parsley. Sauté the vegetables over medium heat for 4 or 5 minutes until they gradually turn into a sauce. Lower the heat to medium-low, and add the spices, salt, and pepper. Stir well and cover the saucepan. Cook for another 12–15 minutes, and stir from time to time.

3. Add the beans and mix everything well. Butter or oil an ovenproof dish thoroughly and place the bean mixture in it. Cover the dish and place it in a 350° oven for 30 minutes. Serve hot.

Fava Beans Ragout

4 SERVINGS

2 15-ounce cans fava beans (or the
equivalent in fresh beans from the
garden or market)

5 garlic cloves, peeled, crushed, but
remaining whole

1 large onion, sliced and minced

6 tablespoons virgin olive oil

1 rosemary branch

6 medium-size ripe tomatoes, peeled
and sliced

salt and freshly ground pepper to taste

1. Drain and rinse the canned beans in cold water. Rinse them again and set them aside.

2. Place the garlic and onion in a large, heavy, cast-iron pot, add the olive oil, and sauté them over medium-low heat for about 2 minutes. Add the rosemary branch, tomatoes, salt, and pepper, and cook over low heat for 8–10 minutes. Stir frequently.

3. After 10 minutes, add the fava beans, stir all the ingredients well, and continue cooking for 5 more minutes. Check the seasonings and serve the dish hot. (Don't forget to remove the rosemary before serving.)

Note: This dish can be served alone, or on top of plain white rice. It makes a delicious combination and provides protein as well.

Fresh from a
Monastery Garden

Fava Beans with Small Onions

$^1/_2$ pound fava beans in pods

$^1/_2$ pound small white onions (fresh or frozen)

10 tablespoons olive oil

6 tablespoons lemon juice

$2^1/_2$ cups water

salt and pepper to taste

finely chopped fresh parsley, as desired

1. Trim the beans and remove them from their pods. Trim and peel the small onions if you are not using frozen ones. In case of necessity, you may use canned onions.

2. Pour the olive oil into a heavy, cast-iron saucepan. Heat the oil over medium-low heat and then add the beans and small onions. Sauté them for 1 minute, stirring continually. Add the lemon juice, water (add more if needed), salt, and pepper. Stir a few times and then cover the saucepan. Reduce the heat to low and simmer gently for about 1–1$^1/_4$ hours. Stir occasionally. The dish is done when the water has all but evaporated. Check the seasonings, and add an extra touch of olive oil and the fresh parsley. Mix well and serve.

Romano Pole Beans and Orecchiette

6 SERVINGS

60 pole beans (the flat romano type),
    trimmed at the ends

1 pound imported orecchiette pasta

6 tablespoons olive oil

5 garlic cloves, peeled

15 fresh basil leaves

$^1/_2$ cup heavy cream

salt and freshly ground pepper to taste

grated Romano cheese for the table

1. Trim the pole beans and cook them in boiling salted water for about 5 minutes. Rinse them in cold water and set aside.

2. Cook the orecchiette pasta in abundant boiling water (add some salt and 1 tablespoon of olive oil) for about 5–6 minutes, making sure that the pasta remains al dente. When the pasta is done, drain it thoroughly.

3. While the pasta is cooking, prepare the sauce by placing the 6 tablespoons of olive oil, garlic, and basil in a food processor and blending thoroughly. Pour this mixture into a large saucepan, add the cream and salt and pepper and cook briefly over medium-low heat. When the sauce is very hot, add the pasta and the pole beans and mix gently.

4. Serve immediately and present plenty of grated cheese at the table.

Fresh from a
Monastery Garden

Pole Bean Salad

60 pole beans (the flat romano type)

6 medium-size ripe tomatoes, sliced

1 small red onion, thinly sliced

chopped fresh basil leaves as garnish

VINAIGRETTE

6 tablespoons olive oil

3 tablespoons balsamic vinegar

salt and pepper to taste

1. Trim the beans but leave them intact otherwise. Boil them in salted water for 5 minutes. Rinse them in cold water and then drain them. Set them aside.

2. Mix together the ingredients for the vinaigrette.

3. Distribute the beans onto six serving dishes (about 10 per person). Place them on one half of the dish. Put the tomato slices on the other half. Place some of the sliced onion at the center of each dish. Just before serving pour the vinaigrette over the vegetables (add more oil and vinegar if needed). Sprinkle the fresh chopped basil on top of each serving as garnish and serve.

Note: This is an inviting appetizer for either lunch or supper, especially during the summer and early fall months. French-style string beans (haricots verts) can be substituted for the pole beans if necessary.

White Beans Spanish Style

(FRIJOLES BLANCOS A LA ESPAÑOLA)

4–6 SERVINGS

5 tablespoons olive oil

1 large onion, sliced

1 red pepper, diced

1 yellow pepper, diced

3 garlic cloves, minced

2 cups tomato sauce, homemade or otherwise

1 tablespoon Worcestershire sauce

1/2 cup dry sherry

1 bay leaf

salt and pepper to taste

2 cups cooked white beans or well-drained canned beans

grated Parmesan cheese

1. Pour the olive oil into a large casserole, add the onion and peppers, and sauté over medium-low heat for about 4–5 minutes. Add the garlic, tomato sauce, Worcestershire sauce, sherry, bay leaf, salt, and pepper and continue cooking for 15–20 minutes. Stir frequently.

2. After the 20 minutes, add the previously cooked beans and mix all the ingredients well.

3. Place the bean mixture in a long, flat, well-buttered baking dish (remove the bay leaf). Cover with Parmesan cheese and place in a 300° preheated oven for about 1/2 hour. Serve hot.

Note: This dish may be served as the main course, accompanied by plain rice. The combination of rice and beans provides a complete protein diet, and is a meal in itself.

Fresh from a
Monastery Garden

Lentils Burgundy Style

(LENTILLES À LA BOURGUIGNONNE)

6—8 SERVINGS

1 pound dried lentils (French, if possible)

2 thin carrots, finely sliced

1 large onion, minced

3 garlic cloves, minced

1 bouquet garni (bouquet of thyme, laurel, and parsley)

3 cups red wine (preferably from Burgundy)

2 cups water, plus more if needed

salt and pepper to taste

1. Soak the lentils in cold water for at least 5 or 6 hours and then drain them.

2. Place the lentils, carrots, onion, garlic, and bouquet garni in a large cast-iron saucepan or casserole. Add the wine, water, salt, and pepper, and bring to a boil.

3. When the mixture begins to boil, stir thoroughly, reduce the heat to medium-low, cover the pan, and cook slowly for 1—1½ hours. Stir from time to time, check the seasonings, and add more water, if needed. Make sure it does not burn at the bottom.

4. When the lentils are well cooked and the liquid has evaporated, remove the bouquet garni and serve immediately.

Note: This is an excellent dish to serve with plain white rice, or to accompany a meat or egg dish.

Beans

Saint Francis Lentils Gratin

4 tablespoons olive oil

1 onion, diced

1 carrot, sliced

1 stalk celery, sliced

2 cups lentils

4 garlic cloves, minced

salt and pepper to taste

5 cups water

2 eggs

1/3 cup milk

1/3 cup bread crumbs

1/2 cup grated cheese

2 tablespoons fresh chopped parsley

1 tablespoon dried thyme (or fresh, if available)

1. Pour the oil into a large saucepan, add the onion, carrot, and celery, and sauté them over medium-low heat for about 2 minutes. Add the lentils, garlic, salt, and pepper, and water, and boil for 30 minutes over medium heat. Stir from time to time. When the lentils are cooked, if any water remains, drain the lentils in a colander.

2. Beat the eggs in a large bowl. Add the milk and beat some more. Add the bread crumbs, 1/4 cup cheese, and mixed herbs, and mix well. Add the cooked lentils and vegetables and mix thoroughly.

3. Butter a flat baking dish and pour the mixture into it. Using a spatula, smooth out the surface of the mixture. Sprinkle the remaining grated cheese on top. Bake at 300° for about 30 minutes. Serve hot during the cold months or refrigerate and serve cold during the warm weather.

Fresh from a
Monastery Garden

Creamy Lentil Soup

4 tablespoons olive oil

2 onions, chopped

2 carrots, sliced

1½ cups lentils

8 cups water

1 bay leaf

1 sprig thyme

chopped parsley, as desired or needed

salt and pepper to taste

1 egg yolk

½ cup milk

olive oil

4 garlic cloves, minced

croutons, sautéed in garlic and oil,
   as garnish

1. Pour the 4 tablespoons olive oil into a soup pot and sauté the onions and carrots over medium-low heat for 2 minutes.

2. Add the lentils, water, bay leaf, thyme, parsley, salt, and pepper. Bring the water to a boil, cover the pot, and let the soup simmer over low heat for 1½ hours. In the meantime, place the egg yolk in a deep bowl, add the milk, and beat well with a mixer. Put this mixture aside.

3. Let the soup cool. Remove the bay leaf and thyme. Then pass the soup through a sieve or blend in a food processor. Return the soup to a clean pot and reheat it. When the soup is hot, add the egg mixture. Stir and blend well. Keep the soup covered.

4. Pour some olive oil into a small frying pan and sauté the minced garlic for a quick second, stirring continually. Let the garlic get golden, but do not let it burn. Add this garlic mixture to the soup. Stir and blend thoroughly. Serve hot, adding some garlicky croutons on top of each serving as garnish.

Beans

Beets

(beta vulgaris)

Though African in origin, it was the Greeks and the Romans who encouraged and expanded the cultivation of beets during the period of late antiquity. Both the Greeks and the Romans cultivated beets mostly to use the green tops, and not the roots. The greens were used very much as spinach and Swiss chard are used today. Besides their use for culinary purposes, the greens were also used for medicinal reasons, such as a remedy for constipation. In some cases, the water in which the beets were boiled was added to wine gone sour, to return it to its original taste.

During the late Middle Ages the beet root became more and more popular. In point of fact, it became, in France, the main ingredient of a soup called *"la porée,"* which was the most popular of all the soups of that period.

In 1757 the chemist Marggraf identified the sugar extracted from beets to be similar to the sugar extracted from sugar cane. Hence the name sugar beet. For this reason, appreciation for both types of beets, the yellow and the red, increased and beet cultivation was expanded throughout Europe. In France alone, during the time of the Emperor Napoleon, 42,000 hectares of beet plantation were exclusively cultivated for the production of sugar for the country. Even today, when roaming around the French countryside during harvesttime, one is impressed to see tall piles of beets on the roadside waiting to be transported to large production plants where eventually they will be converted into pure sugar.

45

Beets

Red Beet Salad with Roquefort Cheese

4—6 SERVINGS

6 medium-size beets

2 apples

1 bunch of mâche

1 Belgium endive, sliced in 1-inch strips

finely chopped chives as garnish

DRESSING

4 ounces sour cream

$^1/_2$ cup Roquefort cheese, crumbled

1 small red onion, cut in small pieces and minced

4 tablespoons lemon juice

2 tablespoons virgin olive oil

a pinch of toasted sesame seeds (optional)

salt and freshly ground pepper to taste

1. Boil the beets for 5 minutes. Rinse them in cold water. Peel the beets and slice them julienne style. Peel the apples and also slice them julienne style. Place these vegetables in a salad bowl and refrigerate them until you are ready to serve.

2. Wash and dry the mâche leaves. Place them in a separate bowl. Add the sliced endive.

3. Mix well all the dressing ingredients. Beat by hand until the dressing acquires a creamy consistency. Refrigerate until ready to be used.

4. When you are ready to serve, set out the serving plates. Divide the dressing between the two bowls of vegetables and gently toss the salads until the vegetables are well coated with the dressing. Serve the beets and apples on one half of the plate and the mâche and endive on the other half. Sprinkle the finely chopped chives on the top as garnish.

Note: This is an elegant appetizer any time of the year, and especially delicious during the hot-weather months.

Fresh from a
Monastery Garden

Baby Beet Salad

12 small beets

12 small potatoes, peeled

16 small onions, peeled

4 tablespoons finely chopped fresh chives
as garnish

VINAIGRETTE

8 tablespoons olive oil

3 tablespoons white vinegar

salt and freshly ground pepper to taste

2 teaspoons French mustard

1. Trim the beets at both ends. Boil them in salted water for about 25–30 minutes until they become tender. Drain them and rinse them under cold water. Peel the beets and set them aside.

2. In salted water, boil the peeled potatoes and onions separately for about 20 minutes. The potatoes should be cooked, but not overcooked, and should remain firm and whole. The same applies to the onions. Drain the vegetables and allow them to cool.

3. When you are ready to serve, place the beets, potatoes, and onions in a deep salad bowl. Prepare the vinaigrette by mixing all the ingredients well. Pour this over the vegetables and toss them gently. Garnish the top with the finely chopped chives and serve.

Note: If the potatoes or even the beets are a bit too big, they can be sliced in perfect halves and served. Whenever possible, however, they should be presented whole. This is an excellent appetizer any time of the year, but especially in mid-summer when the baby beets and small potatoes are fresh and tender.

47

Beets

Beets à la Dijonnaise

1 pound beets, peeled and diced

finely chopped fresh chervil as garnish

SAUCE

2 tablespoons white vermouth

$\frac{1}{2}$ cup heavy cream

2 tablespoons Dijon mustard

salt and pepper to taste

1. Boil the diced beets in salted water for about 7–8 minutes. Drain them and set them aside.

2. When you are ready to serve, prepare the sauce by combining in a casserole the vermouth, cream, mustard, salt, and pepper. Mix well and heat the sauce over low heat. Add the beets and stir continually for about a minute until they are reheated. Serve them immediately garnished with the finely chopped chervil.

Note: Beets thus prepared are a good accompaniment to certain fish and egg main courses.

Cold Beet Soup

2 quarts water

6 good-size fresh beets, peeled and diced

2 leeks, white parts only, sliced

2 shallots, peeled and chopped

2 celery stalks, finely sliced

1 bouillon cube

2 teaspoons sugar

salt and pepper to taste

2 8-ounce containers plain low-fat yogurt

1 medium-size cucumber, peeled, seeded,
    and finely chopped

finely chopped fresh dill to taste

1 bunch of fresh chives, finely chopped

1. Pour the water into a soup pot and add the vegetables, bouillon cube, and sugar. Bring to a boil, cover the pot, and cook slowly for 30 minutes over medium-low heat.

2. After 30 minutes, add the salt and pepper, stir well, and remove the pot from the heat. Let the soup stand for 30 minutes to cool. Blend the soup in a blender or food processor and then place it in a container in the refrigerator for several hours or even a day before serving.

3. Place the yogurt in a deep bowl, add the cucumber, dill, and chives and mix all well by hand. Keep it in the refrigerator until you are ready to serve. Just before serving, mix and blend the creamy beet soup and the yogurt mixture well. Serve cold.

Note: This soup makes an ideal appetizer for a hot summer day.

Beets

Beets Rémoulade

6 medium-size red beets, peeled and sliced julienne style

1 small onion, sliced julienne style

5 tablespoons lemon juice

RÉMOULADE SAUCE

1 egg yolk

2 tablespoons French mustard

$^1/_2$ cup olive oil (more or less)

1 tablespoon tarragon-scented vinegar

salt and pepper to taste

1. Cook the sliced beets and onion for 1 minute in salted boiling water and drain them completely. Place the vegetables in a deep bowl and add the lemon juice. Mix well and refrigerate for at least 2 hours before serving.

2. Place the egg yolk in another deep bowl and add the mustard. Then gradually add the oil as you whisk the mixture with a mixer. Add the vinegar, salt, and pepper until the sauce achieves an even consistency. Keep it refrigerated until you are ready to use.

3. When you are ready to serve, blend the beets and onion with the sauce well. Serve the beets cold as an appetizer.

Note: The beets go well with hard-boiled eggs and tomato slices on the side.

Cabbage, Broccoli, Brussels Sprouts, Cauliflower

(brassica oleracea)

All these vegetables are included here for they are all members of the same Brassica extraction. The cabbage is considered one of the oldest and better-known vegetables of early antiquity. Some claim its origin at least in its wild state to be the European coast of the Atlantic Ocean and the Mediterranean Sea. Others claim the cabbage originated on the Asiatic continent. Whatever its exact origins may be, the truth is that the cabbage and its derivatives were highly esteemed by the people of ancient times. The Germans and the Celts especially were avid cultivators of all types of cabbage and the Romans were not far behind. The Romans attributed certain properties to the cabbage. For instance, they used it as a means to overcome a melancholic state and as an antidote against alcohol, especially before attending the lavish banquets and wild parties for which they were famous and at which inordinate amounts of alcohol were consumed. This tradition survives to this day where in certain countries of Eastern Europe cabbage leaves are eaten as a remedy after a heavy consumption of vodka. In France, there is a special cabbage soup which is used as a remedy after heavy wine drinking.

Besides all these peripheral attributes, the vegetables of the cabbage family are particularly important because they are rich in vitamins, minerals, calcium, magnesium, and sulfites. In our time, there are many theories in the health community which seriously encourage the inclusion of these vegetables in our daily diet as a way to fight cancer. Recent studies have shown that a diet rich in cruciferous vegetables such as broccoli and cauliflower definitely lowers the risk of cancer, especially when these are consumed in certain amounts on a weekly basis.

Cabbage, Broccoli,
Brussels Sprouts,
Cauliflower

Two-Cabbage Salad

(SALADE AUX DEUX CHOUX)

6–8 SERVINGS

¹/₂ medium-size white cabbage, sliced julienne style and minced

¹/₂ medium-size red cabbage, sliced julienne style and minced

4 clementines, peeled and separated into segments

¹/₂ cup sliced almonds, roasted (roasted in the oven at 300° 15 minutes)

¹/₃ cup blue cheese, in small chunks (Blue d'Auvergne if possible)

SALAD DRESSING

¹/₃ cup olive oil

4 tablespoons fresh lemon juice

salt and freshly ground pepper to taste

1. Place the minced cabbages in a deep salad bowl. Add the clementines and roasted sliced almonds. Add the blue cheese.

2. Prepare the salad dressing by mixing all the ingredients well. Just before serving, pour the dressing over the vegetables. Toss the salad and serve it at room temperature.

Note: This salad can be served as an appetizer, or it can be served after the main course.

Fresh from a
Monastery Garden

Creamy Cabbage
(CHOU À LA CRÈME)

6 SERVINGS

1 good-size white cabbage, trimmed

1 4-ounce stick of butter

3 carrots, sliced

1 large Bermuda onion, sliced

2 cups water

salt

5 tablespoons flour or corn starch

2 cups milk

pepper to taste

1. Slice the cabbage into 6 even chunks, making sure that each one remains intact. Place them carefully in a casserole with boiling water. Boil for 2–3 minutes. Drain them carefully so they continue to remain whole. Rinse them in cold water.

2. Melt half of the butter in a good-size casserole, add the carrots and onion, and cook over low heat for about 4–5 minutes. Then carefully add the 6 cabbage chunks and 2 cups of water. Sprinkle on some salt, stir, cover the casserole, and cook slowly over low heat for 25–30 minutes.

3. In the meantime, prepare a béchamel sauce in a separate saucepan by first melting the rest of the butter and then adding the flour or cornstarch and stirring continually until they are well mixed. Add the milk, and salt and pepper, and stir continually over low heat until the sauce is the right consistency.

4. When the cabbage and other vegetables are cooked (after 25–30 minutes), place them with great care in a well-buttered long, flat, ovenproof baking dish. Pour the béchamel sauce on top and cover well all the vegetables. Place the dish in a 350° preheated oven for 15 minutes. Serve hot.

Note: This dish accompanies egg or meat dishes well. On a special occasion, it can be served as an appetizer.

Cabbage, Broccoli,
Brussels Sprouts,
Cauliflower

Monastery-Style Cabbage Coleslaw

6—8 SERVINGS

1 small- to medium-size cabbage, shredded

4 medium-size carrots, grated

6 scallions, finely sliced

1/2 cup mayonnaise of your preference

3 tablespoons white vinegar

2 tablespoons lemon juice

a dash of salt and pepper to taste

Combine the vegetables in a big bowl. Add the mayonnaise and the remaining ingredients. Mix very well and place the bowl in the refrigerator for at least 2 hours before serving. Serve it cold.

Note: This basic coleslaw, besides being nutritious, is an excellent dish to serve during the hot days of summer. It is a good accompaniment for almost anything.

Fresh from a
Monastery Garden

Chinese Cabbage Salad

1 head of Chinese cabbage, sliced julienne style

2 large carrots, sliced julienne style

1 onion, thinly sliced

4 tangerines, peeled and separated into strips or segments

2 apples, peeled and thinly sliced

¼ pound goat cheese, crumbled

VINAIGRETTE

8 tablespoons walnut or hazelnut oil

2 tablespoons lemon juice

2 tablespoons aromatic and fruity vinegar (raspberry or other)

salt and pepper to taste

finely chopped fresh chives

1. Place the vegetables and fruits in a deep salad bowl.

2. Mix all the dressing ingredients well. When you are ready to serve, add the crumbled goat cheese to the salad. Pour the dressing over the salad and toss it a few times to see that the vegetables and fruits are equally well coated. Serve immediately.

Note: This salad makes a good appetizer for a relaxed lunch or brunch.

Valamo Cabbage Soup

I small white cabbage, thinly sliced

2 large potatoes, peeled and diced

2 medium-size onions, sliced

8 cups water

I teaspoon paprika

1/2 teaspoon cumin

a pinch of cayenne pepper

salt to taste

I 8-ounce container plain yogurt
  or sour cream

finely chopped fresh parsley as garnish

1. Place the vegetables and water in a large soup kettle and bring to a boil. Lower the heat to medium, and add the paprika, cumin, cayenne pepper, and salt. Stir a few times. Cover the pot and cook for about 30 minutes. Allow the soup to cool.

2. When the soup has cooled a bit, place it in a blender and whirl it for a minute or so until it is well mixed. Pour the creamy soup back into the kettle, add the yogurt or sour cream, and mix it well with a large spoon. Reheat the soup before serving, but do not bring it to a boil. Serve the soup hot and garnish the top of each serving with finely chopped parsley. (This can also be refrigerated and served cold.)

Fresh from a
Monastery Garden

Broccoli and Tomato Casserole

6 SERVINGS

olive oil, as needed

2 heads broccoli, sliced into florets and
    stem parts

6 medium-size tomatoes, peeled and sliced

1 cup fresh mushrooms, washed and sliced

1 large onion, sliced

2 garlic cloves, minced

$^{1}/_{2}$ cup fresh basil, chopped

2 cups egg noodles (more if necessary)

3 eggs, beaten

$^{1}/_{2}$ cup milk

salt and pepper to taste

$^{1}/_{2}$ cup grated cheese

bread crumbs

1. Pour the oil into a large, deep skillet, add all the vegetables except the garlic. Sauté the vegetables over medium-low heat until tender, then add the garlic and basil. Stir well, turn off the heat, and cover the skillet.

2. Boil the noodles in salted water for about 8 minutes. Drain them and coat them with a bit of olive oil. Set them aside.

3. Beat the eggs in a deep bowl, add the milk, salt, pepper, and half the grated cheese. Mix well.

4. Thoroughly butter or oil a long baking dish, add the vegetables and noodles, and distribute them evenly. Pour over them the egg mixture. Sprinkle on the top the rest of the grated cheese, and then the bread crumbs. Bake at 350° for about 30–40 minutes. Serve hot.

Note: This is a wonderful winter dish and it should be served as a main course. It is a complete meal in itself!

Saint Gertrude Broccoli Salad

4–6 SERVINGS

I large head of broccoli (or 2 medium-size)

salt

I large bunch of mesclun salad (tender salad greens)

6 medium-size tomatoes, peeled and diced

I red onion, thinly sliced

VINAIGRETTE

4 tablespoons olive oil

3 tablespoons walnut oil

3 tablespoons wine vinegar

2 tablespoons lemon juice

$1/2$ teaspoon creamy mustard

salt and freshly ground pepper to taste

I. Put the broccoli in a container filled with cold water for I hour or until you are ready to use it. After I hour, carefully separate the florets and cut the top parts of the stem (the good ones) into thin slices. Discard the tough parts.

2. Place the broccoli in a casserole. Add water and salt, and boil it over medium heat for 6 or 7 minutes. Drain it immediately after that and rinse it in cold water to preserve its freshness and color. Set it aside.

3. Wash and dry the mesclun greens.

4. Just before serving, mix all the vegetables in a deep bowl. Prepare the vinaigrette. Mix the ingredients thoroughly and pour the vinaigrette over the vegetables. Toss the salad with care and be mindful to see that all the vegetables are well coated.

Note: Serve this salad as an appetizer during the harvest months when the tomatoes are ripe and at their best.

Fresh from a
Monastery Garden

Broccoli au Gratin

(GRATIN DE BROCOLI)

6 SERVINGS

3 medium-size heads of broccoli, trimmed

7 good-size potatoes, peeled

1 onion, sliced

olive oil, as needed

5 garlic cloves, peeled and minced

1 pint heavy cream

salt and pepper to taste

a dash of nutmeg

grated cheese of your preference

1. Cook the broccoli and potatoes in boiling water until they are soft and tender. Drain them, and then chop them coarsely and mash them.

2. Place the sliced onion in a skillet, pour in some olive oil, and sauté over medium-low heat for a minute and a half or two. At the end, add the garlic, stir well, and withdraw the skillet from the heat.

3. Place the mashed broccoli and potatoes in a deep bowl. Add the onion and garlic mixture, cream, salt, pepper, and a dash of nutmeg. Mix all the ingredients well.

4. Thoroughly butter a long, flat ovenproof dish and generously sprinkle some grated cheese over the buttered surface. Closely pack the creamy vegetable mixture into the dish and smooth the top evenly. Sprinkle more grated cheese over the entire top and bake it in the oven at 350° for approximately 30 minutes. Serve hot.

Note: This is a good accompaniment for both egg, fish, and meat main courses.

Cabbage, Broccoli,
Brussels Sprouts,
Cauliflower

Broccoli and Pasta San Giorgio

$^1/_2$ pound fresh broccoli

$^1/_3$ cup plus 2 tablespoons olive oil

2 cups rotini pasta (or other pasta of
   your preference)

$^2/_3$ cup fresh basil leaves

6 garlic cloves, peeled

pepper to taste

grated Romano cheese for the table

1. Cut the broccoli into florets. Discard the rest. Place the broccoli in a casserole of salted boiling water. Add the 2 tablespoons of olive oil. After 5 minutes, add the rotini noodles and continue cooking for another 10 minutes over medium heat. Stir occasionally.

2. While the broccoli and noodles are cooking, prepare the sauce by placing the basil and garlic in a food processor and adding the remaining $^1/_3$ cup of olive oil and pepper. Whirl for a minute or two until the sauce acquires an even consistency. Add more oil if necessary.

3. When the broccoli and noodles are ready, drain them and place them back in the casserole, add the basil-garlic sauce, and mix with care. Serve hot, accompanied by grated cheese at the table.

Fresh from a
Monastery Garden

Broccoli Flans

6—8 SERVINGS

3 medium-size heads of broccoli, trimmed

salt

2 tablespoons butter

4 teaspoons cornstarch

2 cups milk

pepper to taste

a dash of nutmeg

4 large eggs

1. Cut the broccoli into florets and cut the stems into 1-inch slices. Place them in a casserole with water and salt and bring to a boil. Cover the casserole and cook the broccoli for about 20 minutes. Drain the broccoli and then puree it in a food processor. Set it aside.

2. Prepare the béchamel sauce by melting the butter in a saucepan over medium-low heat. Add the cornstarch and stir continuously with a whisk. Add the milk gradually. Add salt and pepper to taste and a dash of nutmeg and continue stirring. When the sauce begins to boil, reduce the heat to low and continue cooking slowly until it thickens.

3. In a deep bowl, beat 4 eggs well, then add the pureed broccoli and béchamel sauce. Mix all the ingredients thoroughly.

4. Place the broccoli mixture in 6 or 8 well-buttered standard-size (about 8 ounces), ovenproof ramekins (small bowls or dishes). Place the ramekins in an elongated flat metal pan, add water to cover halfway up the sides of the ramekins. Bake in a 350° oven for 30 minutes. When the flans are done (the flans are done when a thin knife is inserted and comes out clean), unmold them carefully and serve hot.

Note: This dish can be served as the main course accompanied by some small potatoes or other vegetables. It also makes a wonderful appetizer.

Brussels Sprouts Provençal Style

6–8 SERVINGS

1 pound brussels sprouts, trimmed

4 tablespoons olive oil, plus more if
    needed

2 large onions, chopped

4 garlic cloves, chopped and minced

5 tomatoes, peeled and chopped

1 bay leaf

a pinch of Provençal herbs (thyme,
    rosemary, basil)

1 6-ounce can pitted black olives, drained

salt and pepper

1. Boil the brussels sprouts in salted water for about 20 minutes. Drain them.

2. Pour the olive oil into a heavy casserole (cast-iron, if possible). Add the onions, garlic, tomatoes, bay leaf, Provençal herbs, olives, salt, and pepper. Cover the casserole and cook the vegetables over low heat. Stir from time to time, and watch that nothing sticks to the bottom. Cook for about 25–30 minutes.

3. After 30 minutes, add the cooked brussels sprouts, stir well, and cover the casserole again. Continue cooking over low heat for 8–10 minutes. Remove the bay leaf, check the seasonings, and serve immediately.

Note: This dish can be served as an appetizer or as an accompaniment for eggs, fish, or meat.

Fresh from a
Monastery Garden

Brussels Sprouts with Onions

4 tablespoons olive oil

5 medium-size onions, sliced

1 pound brussels sprouts, trimmed

salt and pepper to taste

1½ cups water, more if needed

1. Pour the olive oil into a good-size cast-iron pot or skillet. Add the sliced onions and sauté lightly over medium-low heat for 1 or 2 minutes.

2. Reduce the heat to low, add the brussels sprouts, salt, and pepper, and cover them with the water. Cover the pot and cook slowly from 1 hour 15 minutes to 1 hour and 30 minutes. Check from time to time to see that the vegetables don't burn at the bottom. The vegetables will develop a strong flavor because of the onions and they will be ready when all the water is absorbed.

Note: Serve hot as an accompaniment for meat or fish or a vegetarian main dish. It is a treat when the brussels sprouts are in season.

Thanksgiving Brussels Sprouts

2 cups small white onions or 1 15-ounce
    jar of the same onions, drained

2 cups smaller-size brussels sprouts,
    trimmed

2 cups baby carrots

salt to taste

¹/₂ cup maple syrup

1 tablespoon French mustard

pepper to taste

1. Peel the small onions. Wash the baby carrots.

2. Put the brussels sprouts and the carrots in a good-size saucepan, add water and salt, and bring to a boil. Cover the saucepan and cook over medium heat for 10 minutes. After 10 minutes, add the small onions and cook for another 5 minutes. Drain the vegetables thoroughly.

3. Into an empty saucepan, pour the maple syrup and add the mustard. Stir and mix well. Add the drained vegetables, sprinkle on some pepper, and cook over medium-low heat until most of the maple syrup is absorbed by the vegetables. Stir frequently so it does not burn at the bottom. Serve hot as an accompaniment to the main course.

Fresh from a
Monastery Garden

Cauliflower with Roquefort Sauce

4 SERVINGS

1 head of cauliflower

3 shallots (or medium-size onions), peeled
  and minced

2 tablespoons butter

4 ounces Roquefort cheese, crumbled

4 ounces crème fraîche or sour cream

salt and pepper to taste

finely chopped fresh parsley as garnish

1. Slice and separate the head of cauliflower into individual florets. Make sure that each remains whole and intact. Cook the cauliflower in the top of a double boiler, the bottom part of which contains several cups of water. Cover the pot. Cook over medium heat for about 15 minutes.

2. While the cauliflower is cooking, prepare the sauce by lightly sautéing the minced shallots in butter for about 2 minutes. Immediately add the crumbled cheese and continue cooking for another 2 minutes, stirring continually while the cheese melts. After 2 minutes, add the crème fraîche, salt, and pepper and continue stirring for another minute or two until the sauce achieves an even consistency.

3. Drain the cauliflower and place the vegetable in a warm serving dish. While it is hot, pour the sauce over the florets and sprinkle the finely chopped parsley on the top as garnish. Serve hot.

Cauliflower Italian Style

4 SERVINGS

1 good-size cauliflower with its tender
   green leaves
salt and cayenne pepper to taste
6 tablespoons lemon juice

4 teaspoons butter
5 tablespoons cream or half and half
garlic powder to taste

1. Place the whole cauliflower intact, with its tender leaves, in a good-size saucepan filled with plenty of water. Cover the pan and bring the water to a boil. Cook for 10 minutes, watching that the cauliflower remains firm. After cooking 10 minutes, drain the cauliflower and place it in a container filled with cold water. Drain again.

2. With great care, detach the florets and the individual leaves from the main trunk, making sure they remain firm and intact. Place them in a saucepan filled with boiling water, add the salt and cayenne pepper to taste, and the lemon juice. Boil for 5 minutes. Drain the vegetable and let cold water run over it. Drain again.

3. Melt the butter in a deep and good-size skillet over medium-low heat. Add the cauliflower florets and leaves. Cover the skillet for 2 minutes; after that add the cream and sprinkle over a small amount of garlic powder (to taste). Stir the vegetable. Cover the skillet and continue the cooking over medium-low heat for 3 more minutes. Serve hot.

Fresh from a
Monastery Garden

Cauliflower with Olives Provençal Style

4–6 SERVINGS

4 tablespoons virgin olive oil

2 onions, sliced

2 garlic cloves, chopped and minced

1 good-size cauliflower, cut into florets

1 6-ounce can pitted black olives, drained

$^1/_2$ cup water

$^1/_3$ cup dry white wine

salt and pepper to taste

a pinch of cumin

1. Pour the olive oil into a heavy saucepan (cast-iron if possible). Heat the oil at a medium-low level and add the onions. Sauté the onions for 2 minutes. Reduce the heat to low and add the garlic, cauliflower, drained olives, water, and white wine. Add also the salt and pepper and a pinch of cumin. Stir gently a few times and cover the saucepan. Cook over low heat for about 1 hour. Check from time to time and see if more water is needed. You can also add more wine if you prefer.

2. After 1 hour, turn off the heat and keep the vegetables hot until you are ready to serve.

Note: This is a good accompaniment for almost any sort of main course. It goes well with egg dishes such as a soufflé.

Cauliflower as a Dip for Cocktails or as an Appetizer

1 large head of cauliflower (or more if necessary)

salt to taste

DIP SAUCE PIQUANT

1 8-ounce container low-fat sour cream

3 tablespoons mayonnaise

1 tablespoon ketchup

1 small onion, minced

$1/2$ teaspoon Tabasco sauce

1 tablespoon lemon juice

a dash of paprika

1 teaspoon Worcestershire sauce

or

SWEET HERB AND EGG DIP SAUCE

1 8-ounce container low-fat yogurt

3 tablespoons mayonnaise

2 tablespoons mustard

1 tablespoon lemon juice

1 hard-boiled egg, finely chopped

finely minced fresh parsley, a handful

finely minced scallions, a handful

finely minced fresh cilantro, a handful

1. To make the Dip Sauce Piquant, mix all ingredients well until a smooth consistency is achieved. Check the seasonings and add salt if needed.

2. To make the Sweet Herb and Egg Dip Sauce, mix all the ingredients well until a smooth consistency has been achieved. Check the seasonings and add salt and pepper if necessary.

3. Slice the cauliflower carefully into florets. Place in a casserole filled with water. Add salt and bring to a quick boil. Cover the pot and boil for exactly 1 minute. Drain immediately and rinse in very cold water. Set aside until the florets are completely dry and ready to be eaten. Serve in a dish with one of the two sauces on the side.

Note: You may add other fresh vegetables next to the cauliflower such as radishes, cherry tomatoes, carrot sticks, etc.

*Fresh from a
Monastery Garden*

Carrots
and
Parsnips

(daucus carota)

The carrot, a humble root vegetable, had its origin in the country that today is called Afghanistan. Though already known in ancient times by the Romans and Greeks, the Germans and the Slavs, the carrot received very little notice in history. For instance, the carrot is not even mentioned among the 90 eatable plants in the capitulary called *De Villis,* which registered the names of plants in the gardens of the Emperor Charlemagne.

Around the sixteenth century, the carrot all of a sudden began to surface and receive appreciation, thanks to a certain experiment in Holland which changed the light brown color of the original carrot to orange, the vegetable thus receiving the name of long orange carrot. After that its cultivation expanded throughout Europe, the Americas, and around the whole world, and it became one of the most popular vegetables at the table.

In olden times, as with other vegetables, the carrot was thought to give protection against certain illnesses. In particular, it was strongly recommended to fight stomach and intestinal problems. To this is added today's conviction that carrots are also very useful in the prevention of cancer. Carrots are a source of vitamins A, B, C, and are even more important as a source of carotene, a great aid to the skin and the eyes. Parsnips are related to the carrot family, therefore a recipe is also included in this section.

Carrots and Parsnips

Carrot Timbales

(TIMBALE DE CAROTTES)

6 SERVINGS

8 carrots, sliced
1½ tablespoons butter
3 eggs

1 cup milk
salt and pepper to taste
1½ tablespoons brown sugar

1. Bring water to a boil in a good-size casserole, and add the sliced carrots. Cook them for about 25–30 minutes. Drain them and afterward process the carrots in a food processor until they turn into a creamy puree.

2. Melt the butter in a large casserole and add the pureed carrots. Cook them over low heat for a few minutes, and stir continually so the puree does not burn at the bottom. After cooking for a few minutes (3–5), remove the casserole from the stove and let it cool for a while.

3. Place the eggs, milk, seasoning, and sugar in a blender, and mix thoroughly. Pour this mixture gradually into the casserole with the pureed carrots, and whisk the mixture with the other hand at the same time.

4. Heat the oven to 350° and butter thoroughly six small ramekins. Place the carrot mixture into each of the ramekins.

5. Put the ramekins in a long roasting pan and fill it with water up to half the height of the ramekins. Bake the timbales for 40–45 minutes until the timbales are firm and smooth. Add some water, if necessary, during the process so that the roasting pan is never dry.

6. When the timbales are done, remove them carefully from the water bath and let them cool for 1 minute before taking them out of their mold. Place a small plate on top of the ramekin and then quickly turn it upside down. Lift the ramekin off very gently so as to preserve the timbale intact.

Note: The timbale can be served hot or cold, as an appetizer, or as an accompaniment to the main dish.

Fresh from a
Monastery Garden

Carrot Fantasy
(FANTAISIE DE CAROTTES)

6 SERVINGS

5 tablespoons oil

1 large onion, thinly sliced

3 celery stalks, sliced

8 carrots, cut into thin slices 3 inches
  long, and then again in 4 parts
  lengthwise

1 bouillon cube

1 cup water, plus more if necessary

2 tablespoons cornstarch

$2/3$ cup half and half or milk

salt and pepper to taste

1. Pour the oil into a deep heavy pot. Add the sliced onion and celery. Sauté them for several minutes until they become tender.

2. Add the carrot sticks, bouillon cube, and water. Cover the pot and bring to a boil. Lower the heat to medium-low for 10 minutes, until the water is all absorbed. Watch that it does not burn at the bottom.

3. After the 10 minutes of cooking, when the water is all absorbed, sprinkle the cornstarch over the carrots, add the half and half, salt, and pepper and continue cooking while stirring constantly. Stir for several minutes (6 to 8) until the carrots are bathed in a smooth cream.

Note: Served hot, this is a good accompaniment to a main course.

Carrots
and Parsnips

Carrot Juice

1 pound good fresh carrots
1/2 pound good fresh tomatoes
1/2 cup fresh orange juice

2 tablespoons lemon juice
1 tablespoon finely chopped fresh parsley
or chervil

1. Wash and clean the carrots well. Slice them and pass through a juice extractor.

2. Wash and clean well the tomatoes. Slice them into quarters and pass through a juice extractor.

3. Mix the two juices together and add the orange juice, lemon juice, chopped parsley or chervil. Stir and mix well. Chill in the refrigerator for 1–2 hours before serving.

Note: This drink makes a delicious appetizer with a cool summer lunch.

Fresh from a
Monastery Garden

Orange-Flavored Baby Carrots

6 SERVINGS

1 pound baby carrots, cleaned, trimmed, and peeled

2½ cups orange juice

2 tablespoons French mustard

a pinch of salt

pepper to taste

3 tablespoons butter

4 tablespoons brown sugar or honey

2 tablespoons fresh tarragon, finely chopped or dried

1. Place the carrots in a saucepan. Add the orange juice (more if needed), mustard, and a pinch of salt. Cover the saucepan and cook over medium-low heat until all the liquid is absorbed. Stir from time to time. At the end of the cooking process, add some pepper and stir and mix well.

2. Melt the butter in a large skillet, add the carrots, brown sugar or honey, and tarragon. Mix well and cook over low heat for about 2 minutes, while stirring frequently.

3. Butter thoroughly a baking dish with a cover, place the baby carrots in it, and sprinkle some additional brown sugar on top. Cook in a 300° preheated oven for 15 minutes and serve hot as an accompaniment to the main course.

Note: On festive occasions one may add small white onions to the baby carrots. They could be frozen or from a can if there is not time to peel fresh ones.

Carrots
and Parsnips

Cold Carrot Salad

8 large carrots, sliced julienne style

4 tablespoons lemon juice

10 mint leaves, finely chopped and
   shredded

I small onion, diced

$^1/_2$ cup golden raisins

$^1/_3$ cup mayonnaise, homemade or
   commercial

$^1/_2$ teaspoon French mustard

salt and pepper to taste

1. Place the carrots in a deep bowl. Add the lemon juice and mix well. Refrigerate for a few hours until ready to be used.

2. Just before serving, take the bowl from the refrigerator and add the finely shredded mint leaves, diced onion, raisins, mayonnaise, mustard, salt, and pepper, and mix all the ingredients well. Serve immediately, for this salad should always be served cold.

Note: This is an excellent appetizer for lunch or supper. To present it at the table in an attractive way, place some fresh lettuce leaves on each serving dish and then put the carrots on top. This salad can also be accompanied by some sliced tomatoes and hard-boiled eggs sliced in half.

Fresh from a
Monastery Garden

Carrots Provençal Style

(CAROTTES À LA PROVENÇALE)

4–6 SERVINGS

1 pound carrots

6 tablespoons olive oil

3 garlic cloves, minced

chopped and finely minced fresh parsley

a pinch of thyme

a pinch of rosemary

1 bay leaf

1½ cups dry white wine

salt and pepper to taste

1. Cut the carrots into round, thin slices. Place them in a deep cast-iron frying pan or saucepan. Pour in the olive oil and cook over medium-low heat for about 3 minutes. Stir frequently.

2. Add the minced garlic, parsley, and the other herbs. Add the wine and salt and pepper. Cover the pan and cook for about 15–20 minutes until all the liquid evaporates. Stir from time to time and watch that it doesn't burn on the bottom.

Note: Serve hot as an accompaniment to the main course.

Carrots
and Parsnips

Parsnip Chowder

5 tablespoons butter

1 small onion, chopped

2 shallots, chopped

2 cups fresh mushrooms, chopped

4 medium-size parsnips, peeled and
chopped

2 cups water

3 cups milk, whole or low-fat

$1/2$ cup cracker crumbs

salt and pepper to taste

finely chopped fresh parsley as garnish

1. Melt 3 tablespoons butter in a casserole, add the onion, shallots, and mushrooms, and cook over low heat for 4–5 minutes, stirring continually.

2. Add the parsnips and 2 cups of water, and bring to a quick boil. Reduce the heat to medium-low, cover the pot, and cook for about 20 minutes, until the parsnips are done. (Add more water, if necessary.)

3. Add the milk and mix well all the ingredients. When the soup is near boiling, reduce the heat and add the remaining 2 tablespoons butter, cracker crumbs, salt, and pepper, and mix well all the ingredients. Serve the chowder hot and sprinkle some finely chopped parsley on the top as garnish.

Fresh from a
Monastery Garden

Celery and Celery Root

(apium graveolens)

The celery and its cousin, the celery root, sometimes called celeriac (*céleri-rave* in French), were originally members of the same plant family. It is believed that its provenance is found in the Mediterranean Basin. Both celeries grow well in a terrain where there is an abundance of water and sun. The soil, of course, needs to be deep and rich in compost and other types of natural fertilizers. Here in our small monastery we usually try to import the seeds of the celery root from France, where they cultivate some excellent varieties.

The celery root is considered in France a *légume gourmand*, a gourmet type of vegetable, hence its extensive cultivation in the French soil and its deep appreciation at the table. The celery root is beginning to gain the interest of both gardeners and restaurateurs in this country as one occasionally sees it on the menus of some of the best restaurants. It is also beginning to appear in some of the better markets. For example, this past summer I was delighted to discover celery root in a nearby market in Great Barrington, Massachusetts, where they specialize in gourmet products. It is clear the word is getting around . . .

Both types of celeries are commonly used here at the monastic table. They can be eaten raw or cooked, alone or combined with other vegetables. It is up to the good art and taste of the ingenious cook how to use and prepare them properly.

Celery and
Celery Root

Celery Root Rémoulade
(CÉLERI-RAVE RÉMOULADE)

4 SERVINGS

4 medium-size celery roots, peeled and
  sliced julienne style

4 tablespoons lemon juice

RÉMOULADE SAUCE

1 egg yolk

2 tablespoons French mustard
  (a strong one)

$^{1}/_{2}$ cup olive oil, more or less

1 tablespoon tarragon-scented vinegar
  (or other)

salt and pepper to taste

1. Cook the celery roots for about 1 minute in boiling water and then drain completely. Place them in a deep bowl, add the lemon juice, mix well, and refrigerate for at least 2 hours or until ready to use.

2. Place the egg yolk in a deep bowl and add the mustard. Then add the oil gradually as you whisk the mixture with an electric mixer. Add the vinegar, salt, and pepper and whisk some more until the sauce achieves an even consistency. Keep in the refrigerator until ready to use.

3. When ready to serve, add the celery roots to the sauce and mix thoroughly. Serve the celery roots cold as an appetizer.

Note: One may wish to garnish with some lettuce leaves on the bottom and top them with the celery roots.

Fresh from a
Monastery Garden

Celery Root Mousseline

(MOUSSELINE DE CÉLERI-RAVE)

6–8 SERVINGS

2 pounds potatoes

1 pound celery roots

salt

4 tablespoons butter

I 8-ounce container crème fraîche or
heavy cream

a pinch of finely chopped fresh tarragon

pepper to taste

1. Wash and clean the potatoes and the celery roots. Pull the celery roots apart, and slice the vegetables into chunks.

2. Fill a large saucepan with water and add some salt. Boil the potatoes for about 12 minutes. Add the celery roots and continue boiling for another 10–12 minutes. Drain them thoroughly.

3. Mash the vegetables or pass them through a food mill or use a processor. Add the butter, crème fraîche, tarragon, and salt and pepper and mix all the ingredients until the mousseline achieves an even consistency.

4. Butter a Pyrex dish thoroughly. Spread the mousseline evenly in the dish and place it in a 200° oven. Keep it warm until ready to be served.

Celery and
Celery Root

Stuffed Celery Stalks Gratinée

2 tablespoons butter

1 whole celery, trimmed and stalks
    cut in half

$1/3$ cup dry white wine, add more if
    needed

salt to taste, only a pinch since celery is
    already salty to taste

3 tablespoons olive oil

3 tomatoes, peeled, seeded, and sliced

2 garlic cloves, chopped and minced

10 black olives, pitted and finely chopped

8 basil leaves, finely chopped or
    2 teaspoons dried basil

salt and pepper to taste

grated Parmesan cheese, or cheese of your
    choice

1. Melt the butter in a large, deep skillet and add the celery stalks, wine, and a pinch of salt. Cover the skillet and cook over low heat for 15 minutes. After the first 7 minutes turn the stalks over on the other side, cover the pot, and continue cooking for the remaining time.

2. While the celery is cooking, prepare the stuffing. Pour the oil into a medium-size casserole, add the tomato slices, garlic, black olives, basil, and salt and pepper to taste and cook over low heat for about 5 minutes. Stir continually.

3. Butter thoroughly an elongated ovenproof dish and carefully place in it the celery stalks filled with the tomato-olive stuffing. Cover the top of each stalk with grated cheese. Place the dish in a preheated oven at 350° for about 20–25 minutes. Serve the stuffed celery hot.

Note: This can be served as an appetizer or as an accompaniment to the main course. (It goes well with fish.)

Celery and Carrots with Honey and Mustard

8 celery stalks, sliced

4 long thin carrots, sliced

1 cup orange juice

1 cup water, add more if needed

2 shallots, finely chopped

1 tablespoon mustard

3 tablespoons honey

salt and pepper to taste

1. Place the sliced celery stalks and carrots in a saucepan and add the orange juice and water. Bring to a boil and then reduce the heat to medium-low. Cover the saucepan and cook slowly until almost all the liquid evaporates. Stir occasionally.

2. Add the shallots, mustard, honey, and salt and pepper to taste and mix well with the vegetables and the remaining moisture. Cover the pot and continue cooking for 1 or 2 minutes, being careful not to burn at the bottom. Stir well and serve hot.

Note: It makes an attractive accompaniment to the main course.

87

Celery and
Celery Root

Corn

(zea mays)

Corn may be one of the quintessentially American foods, even as popular today as in the time when Columbus first came to the Americas and the first Pilgrims settled in New England. The history books tell us that corn was served in that first Thanksgiving celebration back in 1621, and it has been a standard feature of the American diet ever since. It is almost impossible for us to think of a Fourth of July national celebration that does not include fresh corn in the millions of picnics and barbecues across the country.

Today corn is not only popular across the Americas but throughout the world; it is easily cultivated wherever the local climate provides good doses of heat and water. Water and heat are essential to a successful cultivation of the corn, as well as good, fertile soil and excellent seeds. The soil needs to be well drained and rich in compost, minerals, and nitrogen.

The cultivation of corn as a grain has become one of the great success stories of American agriculture. Entire regions of the Western states in the United States have become part of what is called today the Corn Belt. We must never forget that corn is grown not only for human consumption but primarily, and perhaps more importantly so, as animal feed. From the point of view of nutrition, corn may be considered of more value to the feeding of livestock than to humans. Corn is low in protein and vitamin B, but rich in starch, providing many uses for manufacturers, laundry industries, and housewives throughout the years.

Corn, in the kitchen and at the table, is principally a summer crop. The local farmers following the tradition of their ancestors remind me every year that corn should be shucked at the last moment just before sitting down at the table. If it is to be eaten on the cob, corn should be boiled for about 3–4 minutes maximum and eaten immediately after. Corn and its derivative, cornmeal, are also consumed in certain cultures as a food quite similar to bread: polenta in Italy, grits in the Southern United States, tortillas in Mexico, etc. Basically corn is a humble grain that lends itself to an infinite variety of uses.

Corn

Saint Lawrence Corn Soup

4—6 SERVINGS

6 tablespoons vegetable oil

2 onions, sliced

2 garlic cloves, minced

3 celery stalks, thinly sliced

7 cups water (more if needed)

I bouillon cube

I red pepper, sliced into cubes

I potato, sliced into cubes

corn kernels from 5 ears, or I 8-ounce
package frozen corn

salt and pepper to taste

chopped fresh cilantro (or parsley) as
garnish

I. Pour the oil into a soup pot. Add the onions, garlic, and celery and sauté briefly over low heat for about 2 minutes until the onions begin to turn.

2. Add the water and bouillon cube and bring the water to a boil. Add the red pepper, potato, corn kernels, salt, and pepper. Cover the pot and cook for about 20 minutes over medium-low heat. Stir the soup several times, check the seasonings, and simmer the soup for another 10 minutes. Serve the soup hot and top each serving with finely chopped cilantro or parsley as garnish.

Fresh from a
Monastery Garden

Saint Martin Corn Soufflé

1 onion

3 tablespoons butter

3 tablespoons cornstarch

1 cup milk

½ cup shredded sharp Cheddar cheese

5 egg yolks, beaten

2 cups well-drained cooked corn

salt and pepper to taste

5 egg whites, beaten stiff

grated Parmesan cheese

1. Chop the onion lightly and sauté in a little butter over low heat for about 2 minutes. Set aside.

2. Preheat the oven to 350°.

3. Melt the 3 tablespoons of butter in a small casserole. Dissolve the cornstarch in the milk and then pour the mixture, a little at a time, into the melting butter. Stir continually until the sauce achieves a thick consistency. Turn off the heat. Add the shredded cheese and stir well. Allow it to cool off for a few minutes.

4. Beat the egg yolks in a deep bowl, add the cheese sauce mixture, and stir well. Add the cooked corn and the sautéed onion. Add salt and pepper to taste. Stir and mix thoroughly. Add the beaten egg whites and carefully fold them into the mixture.

5. Butter thoroughly a soufflé dish and sprinkle the grated cheese over the buttered surface. Pour the egg-corn mixture into it with care. Bake for about 30–40 minutes. The soufflé is ready when the top gets brown and it begins to puff at the center. The soufflé should be served immediately after it comes out of the oven.

Note: This dish should be served as a main course. It could be accompanied by another cooked vegetable in season.

Saint Martha Corn Casserole

6–8 SERVINGS

7 ears of new corn

4 tablespoons olive oil or other oil

1 large onion, thinly sliced

4 large tomatoes, peeled and chopped

3 garlic cloves, minced

finely chopped fresh parsley, to taste

salt and pepper to taste

2 medium-size yellow squash, cut in small chunks

2 medium-size zucchini, cut in small chunks

4 tablespoons water

$^1/_2$ cup grated Cheddar cheese

1. Separate the kernels from the ears of corn with a long, sharp knife. Place them in salted boiling water for 2–3 minutes. Drain them and set them aside.

2. Pour the oil into a large, heavy saucepan and add first the onion, tomatoes, garlic, parsley, and the salt and pepper. Cook over medium-low heat for about 3 minutes until the mixture begins to turn into a sauce. Stir.

3. Add the corn, squash and zucchini and mix all ingredients well. Cover the saucepan, reduce the heat to low, and continue cooking for 4–5 minutes. Stir occasionally and add 4 tablespoons of water to increase the sauce or juice.

4. Butter thoroughly an ovenproof casserole dish, and spoon the vegetables and the sauce into it. Cover the top with the grated cheese and bake in a 350° oven for about 20 minutes until the cheese turns bubbly and melts. Serve hot.

Fresh from a
Monastery Garden

Fresh Corn Polenta

2 cups corn kernels (about 4 ears of new
    corn)

1 onion, peeled and diced

2 tablespoons olive oil

3 cups water

1 cup coarse or fine-grained polenta
    (cornmeal)

salt

freshly ground pepper to taste

3 tablespoons butter

6 tablespoons grated Parmesan cheese

crushed fresh rosemary leaves

1. Place the corn kernels in a saucepan. Add water and boil for 5 minutes, then drain them and set them apart.

2. Sauté the onion briefly in the olive oil over medium-low heat for about 2–3 minutes. Set aside.

3. Bring the 3 cups water to a boil in a good-size saucepan and gradually add the polenta and salt. Stir continually until the mixture thickens. Add the corn then and the onion and continue cooking and stirring constantly until the polenta thickens and all elements are thoroughly blended.

4. During the last minutes of cooking add the pepper, butter, grated cheese, and fresh rosemary leaves. Mix well and serve hot. The polenta may be served on a large preheated platter, in a bowl, or on individual dishes. It can also be kept warm in a preheated oven until ready to serve.

Corn

Corn-Stuffed Tomatoes

6 SERVINGS

6 large ripe but firm tomatoes

2 tablespoons olive oil

1 onion, diced

3 eggs

$^1/_2$ cup milk

2 cups cooked new corn kernels (scraped from the ears)

$^1/_3$ cup grated cheese (your favorite)

finely chopped parsley

1 teaspoon dried thyme, or better yet, fresh

6 rosemary leaves, crushed

a few basil leaves, chopped

salt and pepper to taste

1. Choose firm ripe tomatoes that stand up well. Cut off the top end and scoop out the insides. (Use them for a sauce or discard them.)

2. Pour the oil into a skillet and sauté the onion for about 4–5 minutes maximum. Preheat the oven to 300°.

3. Beat the eggs in a deep bowl, add the milk, and beat some more. Add the corn kernels, $^1/_3$ cup grated cheese, onion, herbs, and salt and pepper and mix all these ingredients very well.

4. Butter a baking dish thoroughly and place the tomatoes in the dish next to one another. Fill each one to the top with the egg-corn mixture. Sprinkle some more grated cheese on each. Bake for 45 minutes. Serve hot.

Note: This is an excellent dish to serve as the main course during the late summer months or early fall, when there is an abundance of corn and tomatoes from the garden.

Cold Corn Salad

4 ears of new corn

1 red pepper, diced

1 6-ounce can tuna fish, well drained

1 6-ounce can pitted black olives, well
   drained

1 red onion, sliced and chopped

4 hard-boiled eggs, chopped

chopped parsley, to taste

VINAIGRETTE

6 tablespoons olive oil

3 tablespoons vinegar

salt and pepper to taste

1. Cook the corn ears in salted boiling water for about 5 minutes. Drain them and then slice the kernels off the cobs. Place the kernels in a deep salad bowl. Add the diced pepper.

2. Chop the tuna with a sharp knife. Add it to the corn and pepper in the bowl.

3. Slice the black olives in halves and add them to the bowl. Add the chopped onion and the chopped hard-boiled eggs. Stir all the ingredients and then place them in the refrigerator for at least 2 hours before serving.

4. Just before serving, add the finely chopped parsley to the salad mixture. To prepare the vinaigrette, combine all the ingredients, mix them well, and pour the dressing over the salad. Toss the salad and serve it cold.

Note: This salad can be used as an appetizer during the summer months, when the fresh new corn is available.

97

Corn

Cucumbers

(cucumis sativus)

This cucumber is one of the plants mentioned in the Bible. We have references to it in the Old Testament in the Book of Numbers, in the Prophet Isaiah, and in others. From the Old Testament we know that the cucumber was cultivated in ancient Egypt, and from there its cultivation expanded to Rome and other Mediterranean countries, including present-day Israel. This is not surprising since the countries of the Mediterranean Basin offer the proper climate for its cultivation. There are some theories among botanists that the cucumber was also known in ancient India and that it might have originated at the foot of the Himalayas. Whether or not this theory has any factual basis, the cucumber is still popular today both in India and China.

There are different varieties in the cucumber family, and most farmers and gardeners try to cultivate in their gardens at least two or three types of it. Such is the case in our monastery garden here in Millbrook. Among the several varieties there are three that we cultivate assiduously every year, making different uses of them. The first is the small pickling variety called *cornichon* in French, and the second variety is the longer, common cucumber grown especially for use in salads. The third variety is a Middle Eastern type, which is perfect for making cold cucumber soup during hot summer months.

The cucumber in general is a vegetable of low nutritional content, and some people find it difficult to digest. However, it is a vegetable so refreshing to the taste that it is difficult to resist it, especially during the hot-weather months. While its nutritional content may be considered low, the cucumber has other qualities that make it desirable in one's diet and for other uses. For instance, the cucumber is well known for its cosmetically value in preserving and enhancing beautiful skin. European cosmetologists and dermatologists often recommend the cosmetic use and consumption of cucumbers as a way to protect one's skin.

101

Cucumbers

Baked Cucumbers with Cheese

4 SERVINGS

2 large cucumbers, peeled

$^{1}/_{2}$ 8-ounce container low-fat sour cream

$^{1}/_{2}$ cup grated Dutch Gouda cheese (or
Gruyère)

a pinch of ginger

a pinch of nutmeg

salt and pepper to taste

butter, as needed

1. Carefully slice the cucumbers in half lengthwise and with the help of a small knife remove the seeds with great care. Place the cucumbers in a buttered baking dish.

2. In a bowl mix well the sour cream, grated cheese, ginger, nutmeg, and salt and pepper until the mixture turns into an even, creamy consistency. (Add more sour cream and cheese if needed.) Spread this mixture evenly on the top of the sliced cucumbers, and place small pieces of butter on the top.

3. Place the baking dish in a 300° preheated oven and bake for 15–20 minutes. When the cheese begins to turn slightly brown, the cucumbers are ready to be served. Serve hot.

Note: This can be served either as an appetizer or as an accompaniment to the main dish (1 cucumber half per person).

Fresh from a
Monastery Garden

Cold Cucumber Soup

6 SERVINGS

3 large cucumbers, peeled, sliced, and seeded

1 leek, white part only, sliced

6 cups water (add more if needed)

a pinch of saffron

a pinch of cayenne pepper

a few sprigs chervil, chopped

salt and pepper to taste

juice from 1 lemon

1 8-ounce container yogurt

finely chopped chervil as garnish

1. Place the cucumbers, leek, water, saffron, cayenne pepper, chopped chervil sprigs, salt and pepper, and lemon juice in a good-size pot. Bring the water to a boil, then lower the heat to medium-low and cook slowly for 15–20 minutes. Remove the pot from the heat and allow it to cool.

2. Blend the soup with a blender or food processor. Pour it into a large bowl or pot, add the yogurt, and mix well by hand. Check the seasonings and refrigerate the soup for several hours. Serve cold and top each serving with finely chopped chervil.

Note: This is an excellent appetizer for a good dinner during the hot months of summer.

Cucumbers

Cucumbers Stuffed with Tuna

2 tablespoons butter

4 tomatoes, peeled and seeded

2 shallots, chopped and minced

5 sprigs of parsley, chopped

1 5–6-ounce can tuna, drained and finely
   chopped

salt and pepper to taste

2 medium-size cucumbers, peeled and
   seeded

grated cheese (optional)

1. Melt the butter in a deep skillet. Place the tomatoes, shallots, and parsley in a food processor and whirl until the sauce is of a smooth consistency. Pour the sauce into the skillet, add the chopped tuna, salt, and pepper, and cook over medium-low heat for 7–8 minutes. Stir frequently. After the sauce is cooked, set it aside.

2. Carefully slice the cucumbers in half lengthwise and halve them at the center, removing all the seeds.

3. Butter thoroughly an ovenproof dish. Place the cucumbers in it, and fill them at the center with the tomato-tuna filling. Sprinkle the grated cheese on top and place the stuffed cucumbers in the oven. Cook at 300° for 20–25 minutes. Serve warm, accompanied by tomato slices and a few olives as a garnish on each plate.

Note: This is a good dish to serve for lunch or brunch.

Eggplants

(solanum melongena)

*L*ike the tomato, the eggplant is really considered a fruit. In the Middle Ages, it was called *Mala insana*, that is to say "bad apple," or "crazy apple." Unfortunately, these ill-reputed names remained in vogue in Europe almost until the fifteenth century. Several scientists of the period such as Leonardo Fuchsius and even Saint Hildegarde of Bingen contributed to the poor reputation of the eggplant. Saint Hildegard, for instance, counseled that one must limit the use of the eggplant strictly to therapeutic uses. She recommended the eggplant as a remedy for epilepsy.

While the eggplant had a hard time getting vindicated in Europe, it literally took centuries for it to be appreciated. Its reputation in Asian countries such as China, Japan, India, and Iran was always excellent. This is no surprise, since it seems certain that the eggplant place of provenance was the Asian continent. Gradually, in the nineteenth century, the eggplant began taking a place of importance in certain areas of the Mediterranean: In Southern Europe, in countries such as Italy, and in Provence in France, and in Spain, where it was said to have been introduced by the Moors. The eggplant was brought to the American continent from the Mediterranean countries, and today it is avidly cultivated in American gardens and commonly used at the table. Now we can find several varieties of eggplants, of all colors, shapes, and sizes, in American gardens.

From a nutritional point of view, the eggplant possesses few calories, being principally comprised of water. Yet, from a medicinal point of view, the eggplant possesses diuretic and anticholesterol attributes, which, in a way, may compensate for its otherwise low nutritional value.

In our monastery kitchen, the eggplant is associated with other products and flavors from the Mediterranean countries, where the preparation of eggplant dishes became an art form, such as garlic, onions, olive oil and olive fruits, tomatoes, basil, thyme, rosemary, and other herbs. Occasionally, I like to try some Middle Eastern recipes where the eggplant is the principal element.

107

Eggplants

Stuffed Eggplants with Tomato Sauce

(PETITES AUBERGINES FARCIES À LA TOMATE)

4 SERVINGS

4 eggplants (small to medium size)	1 egg, beaten
5 tablespoons olive oil	salt and pepper to taste
1 onion, sliced	a pinch of cumin
1 garlic clove, sliced and minced	freshly chopped parsley as garnish
6 sprigs parsley, chopped	

QUICK TOMATO SAUCE

5 ripe tomatoes	a few sprigs parsley, chopped
1 medium-size onion	4 tablespoons olive oil
2 garlic cloves	salt and pepper to taste

1. Slice the eggplants evenly in half lengthwise. Place them in a casserole with salted water for about 1 hour. Drain them, and scoop out the insides of each half carefully, leaving the shells intact. Chop the eggplant insides.

2. Pour the oil into a frying pan. Add the chopped insides of the eggplant, and the onion, garlic, and parsley. Sauté gently for about 2 or 3 minutes over medium heat. Remove from the heat and add the beaten egg, salt, pepper, and a pinch of cumin, and mix these ingredients together well.

3. Fill the eggplant shells with the vegetable/egg mixture. Place the eggplants in a well-buttered dish, cover with aluminum foil, and bake at 350° for 30 minutes.

4. To prepare the French-style tomato sauce, place in a food processor the tomatoes, onion, garlic cloves, and parsley, and blend well. Pour the 4 tablespoons of olive oil into a deep pan, add the tomato mixture, and cook slowly over medium-low heat, stirring often until the mixture reduces and turns into a sauce (about 20 minutes). Add salt and pepper to taste.

5. Place the eggplants on hot plates, and pour the tomato sauce on the top of each. Sprinkle the freshly chopped parsley over the top and serve hot.

Fresh from a
Monastery Garden

Eggplant au Gratin

(AUBERGINES AU GRATIN)

4 SERVINGS

2 good-size eggplants, cut into
    1-inch-thick round slices

salt

6 large ripe tomatoes, washed

1 large onion, peeled

3 garlic cloves, peeled

8 basil leaves

a few oregano or thyme leaves

pepper to taste

olive oil as needed

bread crumbs as needed

1. Place the eggplant slices in a large container filled with water. Add salt to the container. Stir a few times and let the eggplant rest for 1 hour. After 1 hour, drain the eggplant slices.

2. In the meantime, slice the tomatoes, onion, and garlic cloves, and place them in a food processor. Add the basil, oregano, and salt and pepper to taste, and blend the mixture until it becomes a puree.

3. Thoroughly oil a baking dish, and evenly distribute half the eggplant slices. Cover them with half the tomato-herb mixture and repeat the process with a second layer of both. Sprinkle some olive oil on the top of the second layer of the tomato mixture and cover its whole surface with the bread crumbs. Place the dish in a 350° preheated oven for 30 minutes. Allow it to cool for a few minutes before serving.

Eggplants

Eggplant Southern French Style

6 SERVINGS

4 good-size eggplants

6 ripe tomatoes

5 garlic cloves, chopped and minced

1 tablespoon thyme, fresh if possible

6 tablespoons finely chopped basil leaves

1 tablespoon rosemary, fresh if possible

salt and pepper to taste

1½ cups olive oil

1. Cut the eggplants into thick slices and place them in a casserole with salted water for at least 1 hour.

2. Wash and slice the tomatoes. Chop the garlic, and mince it afterward. Drain the eggplants.

3. Butter or oil an elongated ovenproof dish well, and place the eggplants in a line (sideways) alternating with the sliced tomatoes in between. Repeat the eggplant-tomato lines until the dish is filled. Insert a bit of garlic and the herbs in between the layers. Sprinkle the salt and pepper on top.

4. Before you put the dish in the oven, pour the olive oil equally over the surface of the vegetables. Cover the dish with aluminum foil and place in the oven. Cook at 350° for 50–60 minutes. Serve hot.

Fresh from a
Monastery Garden

Eggplant Caviar

4 good-size eggplants

6 tablespoons extra-virgin olive oil

4 tomatoes, peeled, seeded, and cut into cubes

2 shallots, chopped and minced (or 1 medium onion)

1 large garlic clove, chopped and minced

finely chopped fresh parsley and fresh thyme, as needed or to taste

salt and pepper to taste

1 8-ounce container low-fat sour cream

1. Slice the eggplants in 4 quarters lengthwise. Pour 3 tablespoons olive oil into a large frying pan and cook the eggplants for 12 minutes over medium-low heat. Turn them often and add more oil if needed. When the eggplants are done, set them aside and allow them to cool. Then carefully separate the pulp from the peel. Discard the peel and with the help of a big knife chop the pulp finely. Set aside.

2. In a deep bowl, place the cubed tomatoes. Add the remaining 3 tablespoons olive oil, the chopped shallots or onion, minced garlic clove, finely chopped parsley and thyme, and salt and freshly ground pepper to taste. Mix all well. Add the chopped eggplant and mix some more. Place the bowl in the refrigerator for at least 2 hours.

3. Just before serving, take the bowl out of the refrigerator. Check the seasonings, add the sour cream, and with the help of a fork, mix all the ingredients well until the mixture achieves an even consistency.

Note: This eggplant caviar can be used as a dip with crackers or slices of toasted bread. It can also be used at the table as a filling for tomatoes or hard-boiled eggs.

Monastery Eggplant Ratatouille

4 eggplants (medium size)

salt

2 large onions

$^1/_3$ cup olive oil

6 tomatoes, peeled, seeded, and chopped

3 zucchini, sliced

2 peppers, (one red and one yellow),
    sliced lengthwise

4 garlic cloves, minced

I cup (6 ounces) pitted black olives

I bouquet garni (Provençal herbs—this is
    made of bay leaves, thyme, basil leaves,
    parsley sprigs, and a rosemary branch
    tied together with a thin thread)

pepper to taste

1. Slice the eggplants, and place them in a container with fresh water and salt and set it aside for I hour. Then rinse them in cold water and drain them thoroughly.

2. Slice the onions and sauté them in the olive oil in a Dutch oven or in a cast-iron saucepan over medium-low heat for about 2–3 minutes.

3. Add the tomatoes and the eggplants, stir well, and cover the saucepan. Cook for about 4–5 minutes.

4. Add the zucchini, peppers, garlic, olives, bouquet garni, and salt and pepper. Stir well and cover the saucepan again. Reduce the heat to low and cook slowly for 25–30 minutes until most of the liquid evaporates. One must stir from time to time to avoid burning the bottom.

5. When the ratatouille is done, discard the bouquet garni and serve hot, or refrigerate it for several hours and serve cold.

Endives

(cichorium intybus or
cichorium endivia)

The present-day endive was originally a wild chicory until one day, around 1850, a certain Mr. Bressiers, in charge of the botanical gardens in Brussels, Belgium, discovered the process of transforming the ordinary chicory into what he called *chicon de chicorée* in French, and *witloof* in Flemish, (which means "white leaves"). Mr. Bressiers achieved success in this enterprise by cultivating these chicories in the basement of his gardens in dark places, where there was no contact with the light.

Today, endives are primarily cultivated in Belgium and northern France, which supply the world market. Basically, all the endives we eat today in the United States are imported either from Belgium or France. This is why they tend to be a bit expensive at the supermarket.

Nutritionally, the endive contains potassium and other vitamins, and is especially low in calories. This is one of the reasons it is popular among many Europeans who are concerned about controlling their weight. As to its use at the American table, the endive is usually preferred fresh in salads by many chefs. However, it can be used equally well in cooked dishes, as one can see here from some of the recipes. Its fine delicate flavor adds grace and distinction to any dish in which it is used.

Endives

Endive and Beer Soup Gratinée

8 medium-size Belgian endives
6 tablespoons butter or margarine
6 containers of golden beer
3 vegetable bouillon cubes
salt, freshly ground pepper, and nutmeg
   to taste

6 slices of bread
grated Gruyère cheese (or other cheese of
   your preference)

1. Wash the endives well and cut them in half at the center. Slice them very fine and then mince them. Melt 6 tablespoons of butter in a good-size deep saucepan, add the endives, and sauté them lightly over low heat for a few minutes. Stir frequently. Add the beer, the bouillon cubes, and the seasonings. Stir well and cook the soup over medium-low heat for 20–25 minutes.

2. While the soup is cooking, melt a bit of butter in a frying pan and lightly brown both sides of the bread slices. When they are finished, set them aside.

3. When the soup is done, pour it evenly into six ovenproof bowls. Place 1 slice of bread on the top of each bowl and cover each of them on top with grated Gruyère cheese. Put them in the oven at 300°, and serve when the cheese is melted and the soup is boiling hot. In other words, when the soup is well gratinéed.

Note: This soup is a delicious introduction to an elegant winter dinner.

Endive Soup Dutch Style

5 good-size Belgium endives, thinly sliced

2 medium-sized onions, thinly sliced and
minced

2 ounces butter or margarine

6 cups water

2 potatoes, peeled and cubed

1 bouillon cube

salt to taste

nutmeg to taste

1 egg

4 tablespoons heavy cream

finely chopped parsley as garnish

1. Wash and clean the endives well. Slice them lengthwise, into half-inch pieces. Slice the onions and mince them.

2. Melt the butter in a soup pot and add the endives and onions. Sauté them lightly over medium-low heat for approximately 2 minutes, then add 4 cups of the water. Bring to a boil. Cover the pot and cook for 10 minutes.

3. In a separate pot, place the potato cubes and the remaining 2 cups of water. Bring to a boil and cook the potatoes for a minute until they are tender. Once they are cooked, remove the pot from the heat and whirl its contents through a blender or food processor.

4. Pour the potato mixture into the pot with the endives, add the bouillon cube, salt, and nutmeg, and continue cooking over medium-low heat for another 5 minutes to bring to a boil. Stir and mix well.

5. Just before serving, beat an egg in a bowl, add the cream, and beat some more until it is well blended. Pour this mixture into the soup, stir and blend it thoroughly. Serve the soup hot and garnish on the top with finely chopped parsley.

Note: This soup can be served at the start of a special or elegant dinner.

117

Endives

Endives Flemish Style

(CHICON À LA FLAMANDE)

4 SERVINGS

4 large endives

2 tablespoons butter

2 shallots, sliced and minced

2 tablespoons honey

1 lemon rind

1 12-ounce container beer

3 tablespoons heavy cream

salt and pepper to taste

2 hard-boiled eggs as garnish

chopped parsley plus finely chopped
parsley as garnish

1. Clean and trim the endives at their base, thus discarding their bitter part. With a thin knife, slice them carefully in half lengthwise.

2. Melt the butter in a large, heavy skillet (cast-iron). Add the shallots, honey, and lemon rind and cook over medium-low heat for 2 minutes. Stir frequently so that the shallots don't overcook.

3. Place the endive halves, interior sides down, over the shallots and cook thus for about 1 minute. Add about three quarters of a can of beer, the heavy cream, chopped parsley, salt, and pepper, and cover the skillet. Continue cooking over low heat for about 15 minutes. During this time chop or crumble the hard-boiled eggs.

4. When the endives are done, place 2 halves on each serving plate with the inner part in the upside position. Pour some of the creamy sauce from the cooking on the top of each, sprinkle some of the hard-boiled eggs and chopped parsley on the top. Serve immediately after.

Note: This dish can be served as an appetizer or as an accompaniment to the main course.

Fresh from a
Monastery Garden

fennel

(foeniculum dulce)

Fennel is a vegetable of Mediterranean origin. The ancient Egyptians, the Greeks, and the Romans all used it often for medicinal and therapeutic purposes. In the Middle Ages, however, especially during times of famine, the Italians began serving fennel more frequently, and in a variety of ways, at the table. At the turn of the present century, fennel was also introduced into Provence, the region of France nearest to Italy, where it has become a staple of the Provençal table.

Though popular in Italy and southern France, fennel has not fared as well in Northern Europe and in other countries with colder climates, and it remains to this day a regional Mediterranean product. In the United States, it was, of course, the Italians who introduced fennel to the American table where it recently has become quite popular in certain kitchens.

Fennel is a fascinating and quite intriguing vegetable with a subtle flavor all its own. Its light, licorice flavor stands out when fennel is eaten raw in a salad, and the freshness of its texture is a treat to the palate. When cooked, however, fennel changes its character, becoming something of a milder and sweeter taste. When cooking fennel, it is always helpful to add a bit of lemon juice and salt to the boiling water, which protects and enhances its taste. When selecting fennel at the market, it is important to watch for the freshness of the bulb. The smaller bulbs are usually best, for they cook more quickly and can also be presented whole at the table.

Fennel can be eaten and served in a variety of ways. Because of its licorice-like taste, it is a good accompaniment to any dish where fish plays the central role. It also blends well when cooked and mixed with tomatoes, onions, and zucchini, or when served raw in a salad with endives, tomatoes, and other compatible vegetables. When eaten raw, a dash of lemon juice or balsamic vinegar accentuates its subtle flavor.

Fennel

Fennel Ratatouille

(FENOUIL EN RATATOUILLE)

6 SERVINGS

6 fennel bulbs

4 large tomatoes

6 tablespoons olive oil (or more if
   needed)

salt and freshly ground pepper to taste

a few leaves of fresh basil, finely chopped

1. Wash and clean the fennel bulbs well. Trim the stalks and root ends of the vegetable. Cut away any bruised parts. Cut the fennel in even slices.

2. Boil the tomatoes for about 10 minutes, then peel and remove their seeds. Chop the remainder finely.

3. Pour the oil into a deep skillet, add the fennel, and sauté lightly over low heat for about 5 minutes until it is cooked. Add the tomatoes, salt, and pepper and continue cooking for another 5 minutes, stirring frequently. (Add more oil if needed.)

4. When the vegetables are cooked, place them in a deep bowl or dish, add the finely chopped basil and allow the vegetables to cool. Refrigerate the ratatouille for at least an hour, then serve it cold as an elegant appetizer.

Note: It is also a good accompaniment to fish served cold during the summer months.

Braised Fennel

4 fennel bulbs

5 tablespoons olive oil

1 onion, sliced

3 tomatoes, peeled, seeded, and finely chopped

8 basil leaves, finely chopped

salt and pepper to taste

2 tablespoons balsamic vinegar

$^1/_2$ cup pitted black olives (optional)

1. Trim the fennel bulbs and slice each bulb into 4 equal quarters. Pour the olive oil into a large, fairly deep skillet. Add the sliced onion, and sauté gently over medium-low heat for several minutes.

2. Add the fennel and continue sautéing with the saucepan covered for at least 5 minutes. Add the chopped tomatoes, basil leaves, salt and pepper, vinegar, and black olives. Stir a few times, re-cover the saucepan, and continue cooking for 2 or 3 more minutes. Toss the vegetables gently and be careful that they do not burn or stick at the bottom. Serve hot or at least warm.

Note: This dish is an excellent appetizer. It also accompanies a fish main course well.

Fennel

Saint Gregory's Fennel Casserole

2 medium-size fennel bulbs
salt
6 tablespoons olive oil or other
1 large onion, sliced
6 large tomatoes, peeled, seeded, and chopped

4 garlic cloves, minced
2 zucchini, sliced
2 yellow squash, sliced
16 fresh basil leaves, finely chopped
pepper to taste
1/2 cup grated cheese, Cheddar or other

1. Remove the stalks and the outer layers of the fennel bulbs. Slice them into about 2-inch squares. Place them in a casserole filled with cold water, add salt, and let stand for an hour. Drain and set it aside.

2. Pour the oil into a large, heavy (cast-iron) saucepan and add the onion, tomatoes, and garlic. Cook over medium-low heat for about 4—5 minutes. Stir frequently.

3. Add the fennel, zucchini, squash, basil, and salt and pepper and mix all the ingredients well. Cover the saucepan, reduce the heat to low, and continue cooking for another 5 minutes. Stir from time to time.

4. Thoroughly butter an ovenproof casserole dish and spoon the vegetables with their sauce into it. Cover the top with grated cheese and bake at 300° for 25—30 minutes until the cheese has melted. Serve hot.

Grains
and
Cereals

Among the grains and cereals, rice and wheat probably know a longer history than most others. The ancient world was already aware of these as much as 5,000 years ago. Their point of origin, however, remains a mystery that is debated by botanists of our time.

Rice, in particular, is one of those grains that has gained universal acceptance, and has become throughout the centuries the main staple in a number of cultures. For example, rice is the fundamental element in the diet of people in China, Japan, Indonesia, India, and the various countries of Southeast Asia. In China, there is an ancient saying that states, "A meal without rice is like a beautiful woman with only one eye." This saying portrays vividly the place and value attributed to rice in Chinese culture. Many other cultures with long histories attest to the same truth!

The existence of rice was discovered by Westerners through Alexander the Great during one of his trips in the Mesopotamia region of Asia. His soldiers carried samples of rice back to the Mediterranean Basin where it was incorporated into Greek and Roman cultures. In later centuries, the Moors introduced rice to the Spanish kitchen, and during the Middle Ages, the returning Crusaders were responsible for the appearance of rice in French and Italian cooking. The French in particular took to incorporating rice into various dishes, as its foreign origin added an exotic touch to the table. In spite of the curiosity surrounding this grain, one has to wait until well into the fourteenth and fifteenth centuries to see the cultivation of rice extended throughout Western continental Europe, where it has now become an accepted staple.

Today rice is a basic, universal grain which nourishes more than half of the world's people. There are over 8,000 varieties of rice cultivated throughout the world. The Asian countries, as one expects, are the main suppliers of rice to the world market.

Wheat is one of the earliest grains to be domesticated by man. It is the chief grain in the West and is used indirectly through its form as flour. Different types of wheat find different applications: the harder wheats are used to make pasta,

127

Grains
and Cereals

while softer varieties go to make bread. Wheat grain can occasionally be used directly, as in bulgur or other forms.

Grains in general are part and parcel of a healthy diet. With the newfound health consciousness among people today, grains have regained their rightful place in the daily fare of those who strive to establish a healthy balance in their eating habits. While rice and wheat remain the better-known and most widely consumed cereal grains, others such as millet, alfalfa, barley, etc., are increasingly becoming deliberately incorporated into the grain menu by those who seek to achieve a nutritious diet.

Fresh from a
Monastery Garden

Saffron Rice Provençal Style

8 tablespoons olive oil

1 medium onion, chopped

1 red pepper, seeded and diced

2 garlic cloves, minced

8 black olives, chopped

2½ cups basamati rice

a good-size pinch of saffron threads

salt and white pepper to taste

4 cups water

2 cups dry white wine

1. Pour the oil into a Dutch oven, add the onion and pepper. Sauté lightly for about 2 minutes over medium-low heat.

2. Add the garlic, olives, and rice and continue cooking over medium-low heat for about 3 or 4 minutes. Stir frequently. Add the saffron, salt, and pepper and stir some more.

3. Mix the water and the wine in a separate saucepan and bring it to a boil. Add the water-wine mixture gradually to the rice. Stir continually until all the liquid is absorbed. Another way of cooking the rice is to pour the water-wine mixture over the rice and mix it well. Then cover the Dutch oven, and place it in a 350° preheated oven for about 25–30 minutes or at least until all the liquid is absorbed. Take the pot out, uncover, and let it stand for 5 minutes before serving.

Grains and Cereals

Risotto della Certosina

4—6 SERVINGS

1 cup sliced porcini mushrooms

$^1/_2$ cup olive oil (good quality)

1 large onion, chopped

3 garlic cloves, minced

1 cup cooked white beans or 1 8-ounce
    can, drained

1 cup pitted black olives (6 ounces,
    drained)

4 tomatoes, peeled, seeded, and chopped

3 tablespoons butter

2 cups Arborio rice

4 cups water or vegetable stock

1 bottle dry white wine

1 bay leaf

1 celery stalk, thinly sliced

2 tablespoons lemon juice

a few parsley sprigs, finely chopped

salt and pepper to taste

$^1/_3$ cup grated Parmesan cheese

1. Place the porcini mushrooms and the onion in a large Dutch oven or in a cast-iron casserole. Pour the olive oil into the pan and sauté lightly for about 3 minutes over medium-low heat. Stir frequently.

2. After 3 minutes, add the garlic, white beans (these may also be added later, after the rice), olives, and tomatoes, and continue cooking over the same heat for another 3 minutes. Stir frequently.

3. Add the butter and the rice and stir continually. While the vegetables are being sautéed in the casserole, mix the water (or stock) and wine in a separate saucepan and bring it to a quick boil. Keep it simmering afterward.

4. Add the bay leaf, celery, lemon juice, parsley, and salt and pepper to taste to the rice and mix all the ingredients well. Add 2 cups of the boiling water—wine mixture immediately after and stir continually. When most of the liquid part evaporates, add another 2 cups of the water-wine mixture and repeat the process, that is, continue stirring until all the liquid evaporates.

5. Add two more cups of the water-wine mixture and repeat the process until the liquid evaporates. At this point check the seasonings and see if the rice is well cooked. If the rice is not yet well cooked, keep adding more of the water-wine mix until it is

Fresh from a
Monastery Garden

finally cooked. When the rice is done and all the liquid has evaporated, add the Parmesan cheese and gently mix it with the risotto. Discard the bay leaf, and serve the risotto on hot plates.

Note: Serve freshly grated Parmesan cheese on the side for those who wish to add more to their plates.

Grains
and Cereals

Risotto Primavera

1 zucchini

$^1/_3$ cup olive oil

1 large red onion, chopped

2 cups Arborio rice

3 cups water or vegetable stock

3 cups dry white wine

16 asparagus, cut in 1-inch slices

8 ounces snow peas, shelled or frozen

8 ounces fava beans

4 tablespoons chopped fresh parsley

1 teaspoon dried thyme

salt and white pepper to taste

1. Cut the zucchini in half lengthwise. Cut each piece again in half. Cut the 4 pieces into 1-inch-thick slices.

2. Pour the oil into a good-size cast-iron saucepan or a Dutch oven. Add the onion and sauté lightly over medium-low heat for about 3–4 minutes. Add the rice and continue cooking for another 3 minutes, stirring constantly.

3. While stirring the onion and rice, mix the water and wine in a separate saucepan and bring it to a boil. Keep it simmering.

4. Gradually add 2 cups of the water-wine mixture to the rice while stirring continuously. When the liquid has been absorbed, add the zucchini, asparagus, peas, fava beans, parsley, thyme, and salt and pepper.

5. Immediately add 2 more cups of the water-wine mixture and continue cooking, stirring continually. When most of the liquid is absorbed, check the seasonings, and continue to gradually add the remaining water-wine mixture, and repeat the steps until all the liquid is absorbed and the rice is creamy and tender. Cover the pot and try to serve immediately while the rice is hot.

Fresh from a
Monastery Garden

Transfiguration Rice Pilaf

6 tablespoons virgin olive oil

1 large onion, coarsely chopped

12 mushrooms, finely chopped

2 cups rice

2½ cups water

2½ cups dry white wine

1 bouillon cube

1 teaspoon dried or fresh thyme

1 bay leaf

salt and pepper to taste

1. Pour the olive oil into a cast-iron saucepan and sauté the onion and the mushrooms over medium-low heat for about 2–3 minutes. Add the rice and stir constantly.

2. Mix the water and the wine in a saucepan and bring to a boil. Pour the mixture into the rice, add the bouillon cube, thyme, bay leaf, and salt and pepper and stir continually.

3. Cover the pot and cook slowly over the medium-low heat. Stir the rice from time to time so it does not burn on the bottom. When all the liquid is absorbed, remove the bay leaf and serve the rice while it is hot.

The beautiful feast of the Transfiguration of the Lord is celebrated on August 6. It is dearly loved by all monks and nuns, for the light of Tabor, which shone from Jesus' face, sanctifies all those that come close to him. The feast of the Transfiguration is also the feast of the harvest, and we keep in the monastery the custom of bringing in offering to the church the vegetables, fruits, and flowers of our gardens. After the Liturgy, the traditional blessing is bestowed upon our produce, symbolizing that the earth itself is made new by the presence of the transfigured Christ.

Grains
and Cereals

Saint Paschal's Barley Soup

4–6 SERVINGS

Saint Paschal Baylon was a seventeenth-century saint from Spain. As a young man, he was a sheepherder prior to joining the community of the order of Friars Minor at Loreto. He was known to have an extraordinary devotion to the Blessed Sacrament and his humble demeanor was a source of inspiration to his community. His feast day is May 17.

6 tablespoons olive oil

2 onions, chopped

3 carrots, diced

1 celery heart, chopped

1 cup mushrooms, sliced

4 garlic cloves, minced

8 cups water

1 cup barley

1 cup white wine

1 vegetable bouillon cube

salt and pepper

1/3 cup chopped parsley

4–6 teaspoons sour cream

1. Pour the oil in a heated saucepan, and gently sauté the onions, carrots, celery, mushrooms, and garlic over low heat for about 3 minutes. Stir often.

2. Add the water, barley, wine, bouillon cube, salt, and pepper and bring to a boil. Lower the heat, cover the pot, and simmer the soup slowly for 45–50 minutes. Add the parsley, stir well, and turn off the heat. Cover the pot and let the soup rest for 10 minutes.

3. Serve the soup and place 1 teaspoon sour cream at the center of each serving.

Fresh from a
Monastery Garden

Tabouli Salad

1 cup bulgur

1 pound new cherry tomatoes, washed, trimmed, and sliced in half

1 medium-size Vidalia onion, chopped

1 medium-size cucumber, peeled, seeded, and cut in cubes

$^1/_2$ cup finely chopped fresh parsley

$^1/_4$ cup finely chopped fresh mint

$^1/_3$ cup extra-virgin olive oil

5 tablespoons freshly squeezed lemon juice

salt and freshly ground pepper to taste

1. The night before the salad is to be prepared, place the bulgur in a medium-size casserole and fill it with cold water to about half its size. Let the bulgur stand for several hours until you are ready to use it. Just before preparing the salad, drain the bulgur into a strainer, rinse it in cold water, and again drain it thoroughly so that no excess water remains.

2. Place the vegetables in a deep salad bowl.

3. Then prepare the tabouli by mixing in a separate bowl the well-drained bulgur, chopped parsley, mint, oil, lemon juice, and salt and pepper to taste. Mix well.

4. Add the tabouli mixture to the vegetables in the salad bowl. Toss and mix all the ingredients well. The salad can be refrigerated for 1 hour before serving.

Note: This is an excellent salad to serve during the hot summer months or early in the fall season.

135

Grains and Cereals

Jerusalem Artichokes

(helianthus tuberosus)

Around 1603, a certain man named Champlain, a governor of Canada at that time, discovered a root vegetable that was quite popular among the Huron Indians of the region. This vegetable, today the Jerusalem artichoke or *topinambour* in French, was believed to be part of the daily diet of the Indians. From Canada it spread to France and other places on the European continent. The French, in particular, became very interested in this root vegetable because they found that its taste was similar to that of the artichoke. This is why it was known in France by the name *artichaut du Canada,* which in due time led to the English adapting the name of Jerusalem artichoke as the proper name for this vegetable in the English language. The name Jerusalem came not from the city of Jerusalem but from the Italian *girasole* or sunflower. This was appropriate since the flower of the Jerusalem artichoke resembled or was a miniature of the sunflower. Both the Jerusalem artichoke and the sunflower belong to the Helianthus family, which means "flower of the sun."

The plant of the Jerusalem artichoke is a perennial in the garden and one must be extra careful about the place of its cultivation because it spreads easily and overtakes the rest of the garden. Such is the case in our own garden, where every year we face the task of trying to contain and confine its cultivation to a small section of the garden.

The Jerusalem artichoke became popular again in France during the war years, where it was often substituted for the potato. One of the advantages of the Jerusalem artichoke is that its cultivation is easy and simple. It continues to grow and prosper even in times of great drought and in the poorest soils.

Jerusalem
Artichokes

Jerusalem Artichokes Basque Style

12 artichokes, cleaned and diced
olive oil, as needed
1 onion, chopped
3 garlic cloves, minced

6 tablespoons chopped and minced fresh
  parsley
salt to taste
a pinch of nutmeg

1. Place the diced artichokes in boiling water and cook them over medium heat for about 5 minutes. Drain and set aside.

2. Pour some olive oil into a nonstick skillet and add the onion and garlic. Cook over medium-low heat until the onion begins to turn. Stir frequently.

3. Add the artichokes, parsley, salt, and a pinch of nutmeg to taste. Stir and continue cooking for 2 more minutes. Serve hot.

Note: Serve this as an accompaniment to egg, fish, or meat dishes.

Fresh from a
Monastery Garden

Warm Jerusalem Artichoke Salad

(SALADE TIÈDE DE TOPINAMBOURS)

4 SERVINGS

1 pound Jerusalem artichokes, washed and
scrubbed, but not peeled

3 tablespoons capers, drained and chopped

3 medium-size Belgium endives, thinly
sliced

olive oil

balsamic vinegar

salt and pepper to taste

1. Wash the artichokes well and cook them in salted water over medium heat for about 10 minutes (they must remain firm). Drain them and scrape off the peel. Using a thin knife, slice them in even small cubes. Set them aside in a lukewarm oven.

2. When you are ready to serve, distribute the cubed artichokes evenly onto four serving plates. Sprinkle some of the chopped capers over each. Surround the artichokes with the sliced endives. Sprinkle some olive oil, balsamic vinegar, salt, and pepper over each plate. Serve the salad while the artichokes are still warm.

Note: This dish is an excellent appetizer.

Jerusalem
Artichokes

Jerusalem Artichoke Soup

(SOUPE DE TOPINAMBOURS)

4–6 SERVINGS

1 pound Jerusalem artichokes

4 tablespoons olive oil

2 medium-size onions, chopped (or 3
    leeks, white parts only, chopped)

4 tablespoons lemon juice

7 cups vegetable broth or water

salt and pepper to taste

a pinch of nutmeg

1 8-ounce container half and half

1 bunch of finely chopped tarragon leaves
    as garnish

1. Wash and clean the Jerusalem artichokes well. Dice them.

2. Pour the oil into a large saucepan and add the chopped onions. Sauté slightly over low heat for 3 or 4 minutes. Add the diced Jerusalem artichokes and sprinkle the lemon juice over them. Stir and mix all the ingredients. Cook over medium-low heat for about 5 minutes and stir often.

3. Add the broth or water, salt, pepper, and nutmeg and bring the soup to a boil. Continue cooking for another 15–20 minutes over medium-low heat until the vegetables are well cooked. Whirl the soup in a food processor and then return it to the saucepan. Add the half and half. Reheat over medium-low heat and stir continually for 2 or 3 minutes. Serve the soup hot, and sprinkle some finely chopped tarragon on the top of each serving as a garnish.

Fresh from a
Monastery Garden

Jerusalem Artichokes from the Ardèches

(TOPINAMBOURS À LA ARDÉCHOISE)

1 pound Jerusalem artichokes

8 tablespoons saffra oil or other

3 garlic cloves, chopped, plus 1 garlic
   clove, minced

1 8-ounce container sour cream or plain
   yogurt

2 tablespoons finely chopped fresh or
   dried tarragon

salt and pepper to taste

1. Wash and clean the artichokes well. Peel them and cut them into large chunks.

2. Pour the oil into a large, deep skillet and heat it over medium-low heat. Add the artichoke chunks and the three chopped garlic cloves. Cook for about 12–15 minutes while stirring frequently so it does not stick or burn on the bottom.

3. Place the sour cream in a deep bowl. Add the chopped tarragon and the remaining garlic clove (minced) and mix well with a fork. After the 15 minutes of cooking, add this creamy mixture to the artichokes along with the salt and pepper. Mix well, stirring several times. Cover the skillet for about 2 minutes, allowing the artichokes to be enveloped by the creamy sauce. Serve the Jerusalem artichokes hot.

Note: This is good as a side accompaniment to egg, fish, or meat dishes.

Jerusalem
Artichokes

Leeks

(allium ampeloprasum)

The leek was already known and well utilized in ancient times. The Egyptians and the Greeks in particular had great appreciation for it. In Rome, it is said that the Emperor Nero consumed a certain amount of leeks daily in order to improve his vocal chords. During the Middle Ages, leeks were very popular and commonly used in the soup appropriately called *porée*, or *soupe aux poireaux* in French.

The leek is one of those vegetables not only very popular in France, where the writer Anatole France called it *l'asperge du pauvre*, or poor man's asparagus, but also throughout all of Europe. And it is now having the same success in other parts of the world. For instance, it is often cultivated in American gardens, and it is easy to find it in a regular supermarket without having to go to a special gourmet store. Here in our monastery garden, we grow leek plants sufficiently to provide us in the winter months. In the middle of December, when everything else is dead in the garden, the only things that survive the frigid temperature are the tall leek plants, and it is a great joy to be able to still harvest something from our own garden at that time of the year.

Leeks are particularly rich in water and low in calories, and they are therefore an easy vegetable to digest and enjoy at the table.

Leeks

Leeks Flemish Style
(POIREAUX À LA FLAMANDE)

4 SERVINGS

8 leeks (2 per person)
2 cups milk
3 tablespoons flour

1 small 3–4-ounce goat cheese, crumbled
salt and pepper to taste

1. Wash and clean the leeks well. Trim them. Cook them in salted boiling water for 12 minutes, then drain.

2. In a casserole, mix the milk and the flour well. Cook over low heat for about 10 minutes, while stirring continually. After 10 minutes, add the crumbled goat cheese, leeks, and salt and pepper. Cover the casserole and continue cooking over low heat for another 6–7 minutes. Turn off the heat and serve immediately.

Note: This dish makes a wonderful introduction to a good dinner. Be sure you garnish the top of the leeks with some finely chopped chervil or parsley.

Leeks Vinaigrette

8 good-size leeks (2 per person)

3 tomatoes, sliced (well ripened)

I cucumber, sliced

finely chopped parsley as garnish

VINAIGRETTE

8 tablespoons olive oil

4 tablespoons balsamic vinegar (or any vinegar of choice)

I teaspoon French mustard (or any other)

salt and freshly ground pepper to taste

I. Trim and clean the leeks well. Cut and separate the white and green parts of the leeks. Slice the white parts in half very carefully. (Discard the green parts or use later in a soup preparation.)

2. Carefully tie up with a string the sliced in half white parts of the leeks, so they remain intact while cooking. Place them with equal care into boiling salted water. Cover the pot and cook the leeks over medium-low heat for 30 minutes. Drain and allow to cool.

3. When it is time to serve, untie the leeks and carefully place 4 halved leeks on each plate. Surround them on one side with the sliced tomatoes, and on the other with the sliced cucumber. Mix all the vinaigrette ingredients together well. Pour the vinaigrette evenly over the vegetables. Sprinkle the finely chopped parsley on top and serve right after.

Note: This is a wonderful appetizer for an elegant dinner.

Leeks Greek Style

(POIREAUX À LA GRECQUE)

4 SERVINGS

8 leeks (2 per person)

1 cup dry white wine

1 cup water

1 bouillon cube

12 small onions, peeled and trimmed
   (3 per person)

1 bay leaf

1/2 cup virgin olive oil

salt to taste

a few whole peppercorns

1. Wash and clean the leeks well. Cut and separate the white parts from the green. Discard the greens. Place the white parts in salted boiling water and blanch them for about 4 minutes maximum. Drain them carefully.

2. Place the blanched leeks in a casserole and add the dry white wine, water, bouillon cube, small onions, bay leaf, oil, salt, and the peppercorns. Cover the casserole and cook the leeks and onions over medium-low heat for about 30 minutes until most of the liquid evaporates. When the vegetables are done, allow them to cool for at least 1 hour before serving. Discard the bay leaf. Place 2 leeks and 3 small onions on each plate and serve.

Note: This dish makes an attractive appetizer for a good dinner.

Fresh from a
Monastery Garden

Leeks Batonnets

8 leeks, trimmed and each cut 7 inches
long

salt

6 tablespoons flour (approximately)

1 egg, beaten

salt and pepper to taste

bread crumbs

oil (for frying), as needed

1. Place the leeks in boiling water, add salt, and cook between 8–10 minutes. Drain them and dry them with a paper towel.

2. Place the flour in a flat dish. Beat the egg, add salt and pepper, and beat some more. Place the bread crumbs in another flat dish.

3. Roll each leek cane (batonnet) first in the flour, then in the egg, and then in the bread crumbs.

4. Pour the frying oil into a skillet. When it gets very hot, place the leeks in it and cook carefully, seeing that the leeks remain intact and are fried on all sides.

5. When the leeks are done, place them in a well-buttered baking dish. Place in a 300° preheated oven for 15–20 minutes.

Note: Serve hot as an appetizer or as an accompaniment to the main course.

151

Leeks

Leek Risotto

(RISOTTO AUX POIREAUX)

4–6 SERVINGS

4 tablespoons butter

1 shallot, chopped and minced

2 leeks, washed and thinly sliced (white parts only)

2 cups Arborio rice

5 cups boiling water (or chicken broth)

1 cup dry white wine

salt and freshly ground black pepper to taste

$1/3$ teaspoon nutmeg

$1/2$ cup grated cheese (Parmesan, or other as you prefer), plus additional grated cheese for the table

1. Melt the butter in a heavy, good-size saucepan. Add the shallot and the leeks. Sauté lightly over medium-low heat until they wilt.

2. Add the rice and stir constantly for about 1–2 minutes, until it becomes well coated with the sauce and begins to slightly change color. Add the boiling water gradually while stirring constantly. Add the white wine also. Add the salt, pepper, and nutmeg midway in the cooking, and continue stirring.

3. When the rice is cooked, add the $1/2$ cup grated cheese and stir vigorously until it is all absorbed and incorporated into the rice. Serve hot and place additional grated cheese at the table.

Fresh from a
Monastery Garden

Leeks Eliane Anger Style
(Poireaux à l'Eliane Anger)

4 SERVINGS

8 good-size leeks   salt

VINAIGRETTE

8 tablespoons olive oil   salt and freshly ground pepper to taste

4 tablespoons tarragon-scented vinegar

1 2-ounce goat cheese, crumbled
   thoroughly (use a fork)

1. Trim the leeks by cutting off the roots and the green tops. Remove the outer layer of skin. Cook the leeks in the top half of a covered double boiler (add salt) for 20 minutes. When the leeks are cooked, drain them and run cold water over them. Drain them again and set them aside.

2. Prepare the vinaigrette sauce by mixing all the ingredients until a smooth consistent sauce is achieved.

3. When ready to serve, place 2 leeks on each serving plate and pour some of the vinaigrette over each serving. Serve this dish cold as an appetizer.

Leeks

Mushrooms

(agaricus)

The mushroom, though not a traditional vegetable cultivated in the garden, became of importance in daily culinary use, and it cannot be ignored in this collection of recipes.

The mushroom, in its many varieties, has a long history. Its cultivation predates that of many vegetables. Mushrooms have been appreciated for thousands of years and collected and used in the kitchen by chefs of all backgrounds and cultures. The appeal of the mushroom, or *champignon* in French, is universal. The mushroom, some also claim, has healing qualities that make it desirable from a medicinal point of view. Today there are infinite varieties of mushrooms in existence. Some are edible and others are toxic. One must be careful and knowledgeable when going around collecting wild mushrooms for the table. Prudence and discretion in this area are the order of the day. Among the well-known mushroom varieties or "fungi," as the mushroom is sometimes called, are the white, well-known, supermarket mushroom *(Agaricus bisporus)*—which is probably domestically the most popular—the chanterelle, the porcini, the portobello, the cèpes, the shiitake, and, of course, the morel and the truffle, among the most-cherished by good cooks. They are a true delight to the palate!

Though mushrooms are not cultivated in the monastery, they are, however, frequently used in the kitchen. I retain fond memories of walking in the woods with my grandmother picking varieties of wild mushrooms to be used later in the kitchen. That was one of the great pleasures of our Sunday walks, especially during the spring and autumn months. Today when I go back to France it warms my heart to see that this ancient practice still continues to this day. It is common to see people off the country roads or in the woods with their *paniers,* picking the choicest gifts mother nature gives us.

Mushrooms

Mushrooms au Gratin

4 SERVINGS

6 tablespoons butter

20 good-size mushrooms (washed and cleaned), sliced

3 carrots, peeled and sliced into small cubes

4 shallots, thinly sliced and minced

$1/3$ cup chopped fresh parsley

2 cups dry white wine

salt and pepper to taste

grated cheese of your preference

1. Melt the butter in a deep saucepan, add the sliced mushrooms, cubed carrots, minced shallots, and chopped parsley. Stir well, cover the saucepan, and cook over low heat for about 10 minutes. Add the wine, stir thoroughly, and continue cooking until the wine reduces to half its original quantity. Add the seasonings and again stir thoroughly.

2. Butter a round ovenproof dish well, sprinkle some grated cheese over the butter, and then distribute the mushroom mixture with its remaining liquid evenly over the dish. Cover the top with more grated cheese and place the dish in an oven preheated to 250°. When the cheese is evenly melted, the dish is done. Serve immediately.

Note: This dish can be served as a main course for a light lunch or brunch.

Greek-Style Mushroom Salad

½ pound mushrooms

1 lemon (all its juice)

1 8-ounce can artichoke hearts, drained

2 garlic cloves, finely minced

4 small zucchini

½ pound feta cheese, cut into small chunks

VINAIGRETTE

6 tablespoons olive oil

1 lemon (all its juice)

1 teaspoon thyme leaves, fresh or dried

1 teaspoon rosemary leaves, fresh or dried

salt and pepper to taste

1. Wash and clean the mushrooms well. Slice them and place them in a bowl. Add the juice from 1 lemon, toss the mushrooms and set them aside.

2. Rinse the canned artichokes in cold water, and drain them thoroughly. Add them to the mushrooms in the bowl. Also add the finely minced garlic cloves. Wash the zucchini and then cut them into thin slices. (The fresher and newer the zucchini the better.) Add them to the bowl.

3. Add the chunks of feta cheese to the vegetables in the bowl and toss them once more. Place the bowl in the refrigerator until you are ready to serve.

4. Just before serving, prepare the vinaigrette by mixing the olive oil, lemon juice, thyme, rosemary, and salt and pepper. Pour this vinaigrette into the bowl with the vegetables and cheese. Toss them well until equally mixed.

Note: This salad should always be served cold, and mainly as an appetizer.

Mushrooms

Mushroom Medley

$^{1}/_{2}$ pound mushrooms

I 8-ounce jar artichokes

I 10-ounce jar small white onions

4 small zucchini

2 I.5-ounce packages white raisins

3 cups dry white wine

I cup water

6 tablespoons tomato paste

$^{1}/_{4}$ cup olive oil, plus extra as garnish

I bay leaf

a pinch of thyme (fresh or dried)

a few parsley sprigs, finely chopped

salt and pepper to taste

I. Wash and clean the mushrooms well. Chop them coarsely and set them aside. Drain the artichokes and the small onions thoroughly and set them aside. Slice the zucchini into small thin pieces.

2. Place the mushrooms, artichokes, onions, and zucchini in a good-size casserole. Add the raisins, white wine, water, tomato paste, $^{1}/_{4}$ cup olive oil, bay leaf, thyme, finely chopped parsley, and salt and pepper. Cook the medley over medium-low heat for about 20 minutes. Then allow it to cool.

3. Place the medley in a deep glass bowl and refrigerate it for 24 hours. When ready to serve, remove the bay leaf and drain the juice from the vegetables. Serve the medley cold as an appetizer, in individual dishes, and pour a bit of olive oil over each serving.

Fresh from a
Monastery Garden

Saint Odile Mushroom Velouté

(VELOUTÉ DE CHAMPIGNONS)

4—6 SERVINGS

2 ounces dried mushrooms
(porcini or other)

I cup water

5 garlic cloves

I pound regular mushrooms

3 tablespoons olive oil

salt and pepper to taste

6 cups vegetable broth (or chicken)

$1/2$ pint heavy cream

finely chopped fresh parsley

1. Place the dried mushrooms in a casserole. Add I cup of water and bring the mushrooms to a boil for about 3—4 minutes. Turn off the heat and let them rest for 10 minutes.

2. Peel, chop, and mince the garlic cloves. Wash and rinse the regular mushrooms thoroughly. Slice them thinly and combine with the garlic.

3. Pour the oil into a good-size soup pot and heat it. Immediately add the garlic-mushroom mixture and the cups of broth. Add the salt and pepper to taste. Cook the mixture for 7—8 minutes over medium heat.

4. Pour the heavy cream in a blender. Add the cooked dried mushrooms together with their liquid along with the finely chopped parsley. Blend thoroughly and then pour the mixture back into the soup pot. Continue cooking for 3 more minutes and then serve it very hot.

Note: This is a delicious velouté to be served as an appetizer for a good dinner.

Mushrooms

Mustardy Mushroom Sauce

(MOUSSERONS À LA MOUTARDE)

6–8 SERVINGS

1 pound porcini mushrooms

2 tablespoons spicy Dijon mustard

1 8-ounce container low-fat sour cream

2 garlic cloves

1 lemon

2 ounces butter

salt and freshly ground pepper to taste

1. Wash and clean the mushrooms well. Chop them into small fine pieces.

2. Place the mustard and the sour cream in a deep bowl. Mix them thoroughly, using a fork.

3. Peel and finely chop the garlic. Set it aside. Extract all the juice from the lemon. Set it aside.

4. Melt the butter in a deep frying pan. Add the mushrooms, garlic, lemon juice, and salt and pepper to taste. Cook the mixture for about 4–5 minutes over medium-low heat and stir it frequently.

5. After 5 minutes of cooking, add the mustard-sour cream combination, raise the heat to medium, and continue cooking for another 5 minutes or so until the mixture achieves an even creamy consistency. Check the seasonings and serve hot.

Note: This sauce can be used over certain meat dishes or noodles. It can also be used as a dip, and goes well with slices of toasted bread.

Chanterelle Mushroom Salad

6 SERVINGS

1 pound chanterelle mushrooms
   (fresh or dried)

20 sweet almond nuts

16 pitted black olives

1 celery heart

4 scallions, thinly sliced

1 large tomato

6 large lettuce leaves

VINAIGRETTE

4 tablespoons walnut oil

3 tablespoons cider vinegar

salt and pepper to taste

1. Wash and clean the mushrooms well. (If you use dried mushrooms, boil them first for about 3 minutes and drain them.) Slice the mushrooms lengthwise into thin pieces and place them in a deep salad bowl.

2. Slice the almonds, and chop the black olives. Add them to the salad bowl. Slice the celery heart and add it to the bowl along with the scallions. Dice the tomato and add it to the bowl.

3. Wash and dry the lettuce leaves. Place one in the center of the six salad serving plates.

4. Just before serving, prepare the vinaigrette by mixing all the ingredients well and then pouring the dressing into the salad bowl. Toss the salad gently and then place equal portions of it over the lettuce leaves on each of the salad plates. Serve this salad at room temperature.

Mushrooms

Portobello Mushroom Risotto

4–6 SERVINGS

³/₄ pound fresh or dried portobello
  mushrooms

4 cups vegetable broth

¹/₃ cup dry white wine

5 tablespoons olive oil

1 large onion, minced

1 cup Arborio rice

2 garlic cloves, minced

2 tablespoons fresh thyme leaves
  (or 1 tablespoon dried)

salt and pepper to taste

grated cheese for the table

1. Wash and clean the mushrooms well. Slice them thinly and place them in a saucepan. Add the broth and the white wine and bring the liquid to a boil. Drain the mushrooms, set them aside, and return the liquid to the saucepan.

2. Heat the oil in a flameproof (cast-iron if possible) casserole, add the minced onion and the sliced mushrooms, and stir continuously for about $1^1/_2$–2 minutes over medium-low heat.

3. Add the rice, minced garlic, thyme, and salt and pepper to taste. Stir well. Add $1^1/_4$ cups of the broth-wine mixture and stir constantly until all the liquid is absorbed. Add another $1^1/_4$ cups of the broth-wine mixture and repeat the process of stirring continually until all the liquid is absorbed.

4. Continue to cook the risotto at a gentle simmer, and again add another $1^1/_4$ cups of the broth-wine mixture, repeating the process until all the liquid is absorbed. Add the remaining broth-wine mixture and continue stirring at a slower pace, until the risotto turns creamy, the rice is tender, and the liquid is absorbed. (The entire process of cooking the risotto should take around 30 minutes.) Serve hot and add a dish of grated cheese at the table for those who wish to add it to their risotto.

Fresh from a
Monastery Garden

Tagliatelle with Mushroom Sauce

(TAGLIATELLES FORESTIÈRES)

4–6 SERVINGS

1 pound regular mushrooms

2 tablespoons butter

3 shallots, peeled and minced

1 pound tagliatelle noodles

1 8-ounce container heavy cream

4 tablespoons chopped fresh parsley

salt and pepper to taste

1. Wash and clean the mushrooms. Slice them evenly lengthwise.

2. Melt the butter in a deep skillet or saucepan. Add the mushrooms and the shallots. Cover the skillet or saucepan, and cook the mixture over medium-low heat for about 6 minutes. Stir it occasionally.

3. Cook the noodles in salted boiling water for about 4–5 minutes maximum so the tagliatelle will remain al dente.

4. While the noodles are boiling, add the cream, parsley, and salt and pepper to the mushroom sauce and bring it to a boil. Stir it well. Lower the heat to low and then cover the skillet so that the sauce remains hot.

5. When the tagliatelle noodles are cooked, drain them thoroughly and place them back in the casserole in which the noodles were cooked. Pour the entire mushroom sauce over the noodles and mix all the ingredients well. Serve immediately in hot plates so that the dish remains hot.

165

Mushrooms

Mushrooms with Garlic

$^1/_2$ pound mushrooms

5 cups water

1 lemon (all the juice)

6 garlic cloves, peeled and finely minced

4 tablespoons olive oil, more if needed

salt and pepper to taste

a few parsley sprigs, finely chopped

1. Wash and clean the mushrooms well. Cut them in slices, and discard the stems. Place them in a saucepan and add 5 cups of water. Let them rest for 15 minutes, then drain thoroughly. Add the lemon juice. Mix the mushrooms and lemon juice well and set aside.

2. Place the finely minced garlic in a deep frying pan. Add the olive oil, mushrooms, and salt and pepper. Cook for a few minutes over medium-low heat. Stir the mixture frequently.

3. When they are done, sprinkle the finely chopped parsley on top as a garnish.

Note: Serve the mushrooms as a side accompaniment to the main course.

Okra

(hibiscus esculentus)

Okra originated in the African continent near present-day Ethiopia. After a time it spread to Arabia and other Asian countries. Okra was first introduced into the Southern United States in the area of Louisiana and Mississippi by the French colonists who settled there. It gained great prominence in Southern gardens and kitchens, and has become an indispensable staple of Creole cuisine, especially in the famous dish called "gumbo."

Actually, the word *gumbo* comes from the Portuguese language. *Gumbo* is the word for okra in Portuguese. Okra needs a warm climate for its cultivation, and this is why, perhaps, it does not always do well in the Northern states, though I know some New York and New England gardeners who managed to get a good crop of okra from their gardens. In our monastery garden, we cultivate okra occasionally, but not every year. Okra plants need a lot of care, and when they receive it, they are prodigious yielders.

Okra contains vitamin A, but its real nutritional value lies in its interior ripened seeds, which are extremely rich in protein. There is almost as much protein in okra as one would find in, say, soybeans. Okra is also rich in certain minerals and fiber, all of which are incentives for including this vegetable in one's diet, at least from time to time.

Okra

Scrambled Eggs with Okra

4 SERVINGS

2 tablespoons butter or margarine,
   (more if needed)
$^1/_3$ pound okra, cut in $^1/_2$-inch slices
1 onion, sliced
1 long bell pepper, seeded and sliced

7 eggs
$^1/_2$ cup heavy cream
salt and pepper to taste
4 slices toasted bread

1. Melt the butter in a deep frying pan. Add the okra, onion, and pepper. Sauté over low heat for about 3–5 minutes. Add more butter if needed.

2. In a large bowl, beat the eggs well. Add the heavy cream, salt, and pepper. Mix all the ingredients well. Pour the egg mixture over the vegetables and cook over medium-low heat, stirring often. Remove the pan from the heat when the eggs begin to set but are still moist.

3. Serve the eggs hot on top of a toasted slice of bread.

Fresh from a
Monastery Garden

Okra Caponata

1 red onion, sliced

4 garlic cloves, minced

5 tablespoons olive oil

12 okra, sliced

1 large tomato, peeled, seeded, and diced

1 red pepper, seeded and diced

$\frac{1}{3}$ cup water (more if needed)

3 tablespoons balsamic vinegar

8 pitted black olives

2 tablespoons drained capers

salt and pepper to taste

1. Sauté the onion and garlic in the olive oil in a cast-iron pot or frying pan until the onion begins to turn golden. Add the okra, tomato, and red pepper. Continue stirring for about 2 more minutes.

2. Add the water, vinegar, olives, capers, and salt and pepper. Stir the mixture well and cover the pot. Cook over low heat for about 10–15 minutes. Stir from time to time, and add more water if needed. The caponata is done when most of the liquid has evaporated. Check the seasonings, stir, and mix well. Remove the pan from the heat, and serve warm or cold, as an appetizer.

171

Okra

Saint Joseph Okra Medley

4–6 SERVINGS

6 tablespoons olive oil

1 large onion, chopped

1/2 pound okra, cut in 1-inch-thick slices

4 cherry peppers, seeded and sliced

4 garlic cloves, minced

1 celery stalk, sliced

1 cup water or vegetable stock

1 cup dry white wine (more if needed)

1 bay leaf

8 small new potatoes, peeled and sliced in half

2 teaspoons paprika

2 teaspoons dried thyme

salt and pepper to taste

1. Pour the olive oil into a large skillet. Add the onion, okra, peppers, garlic, and celery and sauté lightly over medium-low heat for about 4–5 minutes until the vegetables are tender. Stir the mixture frequently.

2. Add the water, wine, bay leaf, potatoes, paprika, thyme, and salt and pepper. Stir and cover the skillet. Reduce the heat to low and simmer gently, stirring from time to time, for about 30–40 minutes. Check the seasonings and add more wine if liquid is needed. Remove the bay leaf and serve hot.

Fresh from a Monastery Garden

Bill Tarbox's Okra in Tomato Sauce

4–6 SERVINGS

1 pound okra, trimmed and cut in
 ¹/₂-inch-thick slices

4 tablespoons olive oil

4 tomatoes, peeled and cut in chunks

1 onion, thinly sliced

salt and pepper to taste

chopped fresh parsley as garnish

1. Place the okra in a saucepan filled with water. Bring to a boil and cook for about 4–5 minutes. Drain them and rinse them in cold water. Set the okra aside.

2. Pour the olive oil into a large skillet or saucepan. Add the tomato chunks and sliced onion. Cook over medium-low heat for about 5 minutes until this turns into a chunky sauce. Add the drained okra slices, salt, and pepper and continue cooking for another 2–3 minutes, while stirring continually.

3. Add some freshly chopped parsley on top as garnish. Serve hot as a side dish to the main course.

Okra

Onions

(allium cepa)

$\mathcal{L}$ike potatoes, onions also have a universal appeal, and are known to be used in culinary concoctions in cultures across the entire world. It is unthinkable to try to find a kitchen in which onions are not used.

The onion and its many varieties belong to the same species of the lily family. The earliest known species seem to have originated in the western part of Asia, in the region that is today Pakistan and Iran. From Asia, the onion spread to Egypt, where it was held in such esteem that it was considered a sacred fruit, something deserved only by the gods. From Egypt, the onion was exported to Greece and Rome. While the Greeks seemed to have had a certain disdain for the onion, due to its sting and odor, the Romans on the other hand developed a great appreciation and attachment to it. The cultivation of the onion was encouraged and fostered throughout the Roman Empire—the Romans believed that the onion gave extra strength and energy to its soldiers on the battlefield.

During the Middle Ages, the onion was given a special honor at the table, where kings and noblemen sang of the magic qualities of the onion and delighted of its inclusion in the most elaborate dishes. As if its culinary qualifications were not enough, the onion was also greatly appreciated for medicinal and therapeutic uses, especially as a laxative.

Today, the onion is recognized as a good source of vitamins B_1 and B_2, and also vitamin C. The green tops of onions, like scallions, should not be easily discarded by cooks, for a great deal of the onion vitamins resides precisely in their green leaves. This is one more reason, for those who can, to cultivate onions in your own garden; you can thus benefit from eating them fresh and whole, green parts included, partaking of all their vitamins.

Garlic, shallot, scallion, chive, and their related cousins all belong to the same general family as the onion *(Allium)*. These are very useful spices, flavoring agents, and garnishes. They can be used in a great many varieties of dishes, and appear in a number of recipes scattered throughout the book.

177

Onions

Onion Tart
(TARTE AUX OIGNONS)

6 SERVINGS

PASTRY SHELL (PÂTE BRISÉE)

1 egg

1 cup flour

1 stick of butter or margarine

5 tablespoons ice water

a pinch of salt

FILLING

1 pound onions, sliced

3 tablespoons butter

2 eggs

1 8-ounce container half and half or heavy cream (your preference)

salt and pepper to taste

1. Prepare the pastry shell by mixing all the ingredients needed for it in a deep bowl. Use both a fork and your hands in mixing the ingredients well until the dough comes together. Do not overwork. Form a ball with the dough and sprinkle with flour. Place the ball in a bowl, cover, and let it rest in the refrigerator for 1 hour.

2. While the dough is in the refrigerator, prepare the filling. Peel and slice the onions. Melt the butter in a deep skillet, add the onions, and cook them over low heat. Stir them often with a spatula. Cool for 8–10 minutes until the onions turn a golden color.

3. When the dough is ready to be worked, sprinkle sufficient flour over the work area and gently roll the dough out, extending it in every direction. Using butter, thoroughly grease a tart pan and carefully place the rolled dough into it. (The dough must be handled with the fingers at all times.) Trim the edges in a decorative manner, cover the pastry shell with aluminum foil, and place it in the oven at 250° for 10–20 minutes.

4. Beat the eggs in a deep bowl, add the half and half or heavy cream, salt, and pepper, and continue beating until the mixture is well blended. Add the cooked onions and again, mix all well.

Fresh from a
Monastery Garden

5. Pour the egg-onion mixture into the pastry shell and place it in the oven at 300°. Bake the tart for 25–30 minutes. Serve it hot.

Note: This dish is sometimes served as an appetizer but there is no reason why it could not be served as the main course, especially for brunch or dinner.

Onions

Glazed Onions

4 SERVINGS

$^1/_2$ pound small new onions

2 tablespoons butter

2 tablespoons Calvados liqueur

a pinch of salt

a pinch of sugar

1. Peel the new onions carefully so they remain intact. Place them in a deep frying pan, and add sufficient water to cover the tops of the onions. Bring the water to a boil and cover the pan. Cook thus for 5 minutes.

2. After 5 minutes, lower the heat to low, add the butter, Calvados, salt, and sugar. Mix well and cover the pot. Stir from time to time so that the onions are well coated with the butter. Allow all the water to evaporate and serve immediately.

Note: These delicious new onions make a wonderful accompaniment to the main course and are very easy to prepare.

Fresh from a
Monastery Garden

Onion Salad

(OIGNONS EN SALADE)

4–6 SERVINGS

1 pound medium-size new onions (Vidalia are ideal)

lettuce leaves

VINAIGRETTE

8 tablespoons olive oil

4 tablespoons fruity raspberry vinegar (or another)

1 tablespoon French mustard

salt and pepper to taste

1. Preheat the oven to 350°. Place the onions whole and without peeling them in the oven for 30 minutes. After that, take them out and allow them to cool.

2. With the help of a small pointed knife, peel the onions carefully so that they remain intact. When they are all peeled, slice them in half lengthwise.

3. Prepare the vinaigrette by mixing all the ingredients well.

4. On each individual plate, place 2 lettuce leaves. Add 3 or 4 onion halves on top. Pour the vinaigrette over them and serve. (You may add 2 tomato slices and a few olives to each serving for extra color.)

Note: This is an intriguing and original appetizer and should be served to guests when one is sure they love onions. The onions cooked this way can also be served as an accompaniment for fish or poultry.

Onions

Onion Soup Gratinée

(SOUPE À L'OIGNON GRATINÉE)

6 SERVINGS

6 white onions

2 red onions

¹/₂ stick of butter or the equivalent in
olive oil (about 6 tablespoons)

2 tablespoons cornstarch

6 cups water or stock of your preference

6 tablespoons French brandy

4 bouillon cubes (if soup stock is not
used)

salt and pepper to taste

a pinch of thyme

6 slices of bread

grated Gruyère cheese or other cheese of
your preference

1. Peel and cut all the onions into slices. Melt the butter in a soup pot and cook the onions slowly over low heat until they begin to turn brown. Stir the onions continually.

2. Add the cornstarch. Stir the onions and mix them well. Add the water or stock. Add the brandy and bouillon cubes. Bring the soup to a boil. Boil for 5 minutes, add the salt and pepper, a pinch of thyme, and then lower the heat to low and simmer for 10 more minutes.

3. Pour the soup into ovenproof soup bowls. Add a slice of bread on top, cover the entire surface of the bowl with the grated cheese, and carefully place the bowls in an oven preheated to 300° for 5–10 minutes until all the cheese melts and begins to bubble. Serve immediately.

Fresh from a
Monastery Garden

Peas

(pisum sativum)

$\mathcal{T}$hrough certain archaeological studies undertaken recently, it has been discovered that peas already existed in 10,000 B.C. The pea is perhaps one of the most ancient vegetables known today. Peas are said to have originated in the Orient, in Persia, the area known today as Iran. From there, the pea gradually traveled to Asia Minor (present-day Turkey), Palestine, and then to Greece and Rome. The humble pea served many purposes throughout the centuries, including its role in England during the Middle Ages as a form of salary for the poor. In later times, the pea became a very fashionable vegetable to be served at the table, especially during the reign of King Louis XIV, who was extremely fond of peas.

There are a great many varieties of peas belonging to the same family. Here in the monastery, we cultivate two types: the tender, sweet snow peas, which can be eaten whole in their shells, and the well-known peas that need to be extracted from their shells prior to being eaten. Both, of course, are readily found at the supermarket. In the monastery, peas are planted in the garden very early in the season. As a matter of fact, there is an old monastic tradition of planting the first peas in the garden on March 25, the feast of the Annunciation and of Christ's Incarnation. Peas in general do well in cool weather, so planting in early spring creates the wonderful result of being able to harvest fresh peas for the table by early June. Later in the year, in early August to be precise, we plant peas for the autumn harvest.

Peas are rich in vitamins B, C, and E. They are also rich in protein and carbohydrates, which gives them a high overall nutritional value.

There is another variety of pea which does not belong to the same family as the ones above, but whose recipes I included here because of their close resemblance. This is the chickpea. The chickpea, or *pois chiche* in French, belongs to the *Cicer arietinum* family, and like the pea is also a vegetable of great antiquity. It was greatly esteemed and thus cultivated by the Romans in their gardens. The chickpea has remained a constant favorite of the Mediterranean countries where elaborate culinary recipes have been created around it.

Peas

Farm-Style Sweet Peas
(PETIT POIS FERMIÈRES)

4—6 SERVINGS

10 ounces sweet peas, fresh or frozen

12 small white onions

4 small new carrots

4 tablespoons butter

6 lettuce leaves, finely sliced

1 tablespoon sugar

salt and pepper to taste

finely chopped fresh parsley as garnish

1. Trim the peas and remove them from their pods (or use frozen ones). Peel the onions and carrots. Slice the carrots the usual way, into circles.

2. Pour water into a saucepan, add the onions and carrots and bring the water to a boil. Lower the heat to medium-low and cook for about 6—8 minutes.

3. After 6 or 7 minutes of cooking, add the shelled peas, butter, lettuce, sugar, and salt. Mix well and continue cooking for about 10 more minutes. When the vegetables are done and are ready to be served, drain and place them in a bowl. Check the seasonings, add the pepper, and toss the vegetables gently. Sprinkle the finely chopped parsley on top as garnish and serve.

Note: This is an excellent dish to serve all year round but especially during the late spring or early summer months when the peas are harvested from the garden.

Fresh from a
Monastery Garden

Creamy Split Pea Soup

1 1/2 cups dried split peas

3 carrots, diced

2 leeks, white parts only, sliced

1 onion, sliced

8 cups water (more if needed)

1 ounce butter

1/2 cup milk (low-fat may be used)

salt and pepper to taste

a pinch of nutmeg

croutons as garnish

1. Place the peas, carrots, leeks, and onion in a large-size soup kettle. Add the water and bring it to a boil. Lower the heat to medium-low, cover the kettle, and continue the cooking for 30 minutes. Remove the soup from the heat and allow it to cool.

2. Blend the soup thoroughly with the help of a blender or food processor. Pour the soup back into the kettle and reheat it. Add the butter, milk, and seasonings, including the nutmeg. Mix well and stir the soup several times. Serve it hot and top each serving with croutons as garnish.

Peas

Snow Peas Chinese Style

4–6 SERVINGS

8 dried Chinese mushrooms (any dried mushrooms can be substituted)

¹/₂ pound fresh snow peas

4 tablespoons vegetable oil

I 4-ounce can bamboo shoots, drained and sliced

salt to taste

I¹/₂ tablespoons soy sauce

I teaspoon sugar

I bunch of chives, finely chopped, as garnish

1. Soak the mushrooms in warm water for ¹/₂ hour. Slice them evenly and discard the stems.

2. Wash the snow peas, trim the ends and strings. Place them in a casserole with water. Bring the water to a boil, cover the pot, and turn off the heat. Let the snow peas rest for I0 minutes. Drain them after I0 minutes.

3. Pour 2 tablespoons of oil into a wok or deep frying pan. Add the snow peas and stir continually for 30–40 seconds. Remove them and set them aside.

4. Pour the remaining 2 tablespoons of oil into the wok or frying pan, add the mushrooms and bamboo shoots, salt, soy sauce, and sugar. Cook the mixture for a minute or two, while stirring constantly. Add the snow peas, mix well, and serve hot. Garnish on top with finely chopped chives.

Chickpea Salad

2 cups cooked chickpeas, or 2 15-ounce cans chickpeas, drained and rinsed

4 carrots, finely grated (in a food processor)

1 medium-size onion, chopped and minced

2 celery stalks, thinly sliced

chopped fresh mint leaves (optional)

DRESSING

1/3 cup olive oil

4 tablespoons lemon juice

Salt and pepper to taste

1. Place the chickpeas in a deep salad bowl. Add the grated carrots, onion, and sliced celery. Mix them well and place the bowl in the refrigerator for at least 1 hour.

2. Before serving, prepare the salad dressing by mixing all the ingredients well. Pour the dressing into the salad bowl, add the chopped mint, toss the salad gently a few times, and serve immediately.

Note: This is a good salad to serve throughout the summer months.

Peas

Peppers

(capsicum annuum)

There are endless varieties of peppers around the world. Some originated in Asia and in India to be precise. But the majority of them originated here, on the vast American continent, and were said to be discovered first by Christopher Columbus in the region known today as Central America. Columbus, according to the writer Pierre Marty, discovered the pepper during his first trip to the Americas. He then took it with him back to Spain to show the Spaniards the sort of fruit-vegetable that formed part of the diet of the indigenous peoples. The type of pepper that Columbus imported to Europe was hot and spicy, probably some sort of the so-called "chile pepper." It immediately was adopted by the Spaniards as a new source of spice for their dishes, and given the name *pimento* in Spanish (*piment* or *poivron* in French). From there on the pepper has become, across all cultures, the most used product to spice a dish. Just think of the regular ground black pepper used in almost every culinary recipe. What could we do without it? The same can be said of cayenne, paprika, and white pepper. There is no doubt in people's minds that pepper has become today the most universal of all spices, helping to enhance the most simple and the most complex dish.

The large-size peppers are said to be originally from Brazil, and from there its cultivation was extended to Portugal and other regions of the world. These large-size peppers, which are very popular and colorful in our supermarkets, can be green, yellow, and red. There is also the elongated light green type of sweet bell pepper. This type is very popular in Italy where they are often used for frying. The sweet bell pepper is also increasing in popularity in American gardens and at the table. In our monastery garden it is one of the few types of peppers cultivated annually. Others include the large dark green pepper and some of the small spicy ones, which I often use in pickling and for flavoring certain dips and dishes.

Peppers, besides being used principally as a source of spice, are also rich in vitamins A, B, B_2, and E. Peppers are also used as coloring sources for many dishes. In certain regions of the world the use of peppers is encouraged in the diet of those fighting rheumatism. Peppers in general are low in calories, but their nutritional value diminishes when they are eaten cooked.

Peppers

Red Pepper Light Sauce
(COULIS DE POIVRON ROUGE)

6–8 SERVINGS

4 sweet red peppers

6 tablespoons olive oil (or more, as
  needed)

fresh parsley, chopped (optional)

LIGHT WHITE SAUCE

2 tablespoons cornstarch

1½ cups milk

2 tablespoons butter

salt and pepper to taste

a dash of nutmeg

1. Cut each pepper into 4 quarters and remove the seeds. Place in an aluminum dish under the broiler until they begin to burn. Allow them to cool and then peel them.

2. Place the peeled peppers in a food processor, add 6 tablespoons of olive oil (or more, if you wish), and blend thoroughly until this turns into a smooth consistent sauce. (You may add chopped parsley for a bit of extra taste.)

3. Prepare the Light White Sauce by dissolving the cornstarch in the milk. Then melt the butter in a saucepan. When the butter begins foaming, add the milk-cornstarch mixture, and stir assiduously. Add the salt and pepper to taste and a dash of nutmeg. Continue to stir until the sauce thickens. The sauce is ready when it is smooth and thick.

4. Add the red pepper sauce to the white sauce and blend them and mix them thoroughly. Serve hot over fish, certain vegetables, even certain meats, plain rice, or on the top of an omelet.

Note: You can substitute 1½ cups heavy cream for the Light White Sauce if you wish a lighter sauce. Heat the heavy cream to boiling point, add the red pepper sauce and some freshly ground pepper, and mix it well. This makes a lighter smoother sauce or coulis.

Fresh from a
Monastery Garden

Red Pepper and Mesclun Salad

4 large red peppers

1 medium-size white onion, thinly sliced

1½-pound bunch of mesclun (tender salad greens), washed, trimmed, and drained

1 small radicchio, sliced into strips lengthwise

8 ounces mozzarella cheese, thinly sliced, as garnish

VINAIGRETTE

¼ cup extra-virgin olive oil

3 tablespoons wine vinegar

salt and pepper to taste

1. Bake at 350° or broil the peppers for about 20 minutes, stirring and moving them around from time to time. When they are done, allow them to cool in a closed paper bag. When they are cool, peel and open the peppers and remove the seeds. Then slice the peppers lengthwise into strips.

2. Place the peppers in a deep salad bowl. Add the onion, mesclun, and strips of radicchio, and mix them.

3. Just before serving, prepare the vinaigrette. Mix together all of the ingredients, pour the dressing over the salad, and toss it gently. Serve it in individual plates and top each serving with slices of mozzarella cheese as garnish.

Note: This is an elegant appetizer at any time of the year.

Yellow and Red Pepper Salad

2 good-size yellow peppers, cored and
    seeded

2 good-size red peppers, cored and seeded

1 pound green beans (haricots verts, the
    thinner the better)

1 red onion, thinly sliced

finely chopped fresh parsley

VINAIGRETTE

$^1/_3$ cup extra-virgin olive oil

2 tablespoons balsamic vinegar

1 teaspoon fresh lemon juice

1 teaspoon Dijon mustard

salt and freshly ground pepper to taste

1. Slice the peppers lengthwise into thin strips. Blanch the peppers in boiling water for about $^1/_2$ minute. Drain them immediately after and run cold water over them to regain their freshness and bright colors. Set them aside.

2. Cut the ends off the green beans and be sure to trim them of any leftover strings. Boil in salted water for the space of 5 minutes, and then drain them and again run cold water over them as for the peppers. Set them aside.

3. Prepare the vinaigrette by mixing all the ingredients well. When ready to serve, place the vegetables in a salad bowl. Pour the vinaigrette over them and add the finely chopped parsley. Gently toss the salad until the vegetables and vinaigrette are well mixed. Serve immediately.

Note: This is an excellent dish to serve as an appetizer for a dinner or even lunch or brunch.

Peppers with Tuna Fish
(LES POIVRONS AU THON)

2 large red peppers

2 large yellow peppers

6 tablespoons extra-virgin olive oil

4 tablespoons lemon juice

2 garlic cloves, peeled and minced

salt and pepper to taste

1 6-ounce can tuna fish, drained and crumbled

16 black olives, pitted and chopped

16 whole capers

finely chopped fresh basil as garnish

1. Slice the peppers in perfect halves, lengthwise. Trim the ends and discard the seeds. Place them in a long aluminum dish and put them under the broiler for 15 or 20 minutes until they begin to turn black. Allow them to cool, then peel them, watching carefully that the halves remain intact.

2. Pour the olive oil into a bowl. Add the lemon juice, minced garlic, and salt and pepper to taste. Mix well and place in the refrigerator for at least 45 minutes.

3. When ready to serve, take the bowl from the refrigerator, add the crumbled tuna fish, chopped black olives, and capers and mix them all well. Check the seasonings and if needed, adjust them.

4. On four individual dishes, place one half of a roasted red pepper and, beside it, one half of a roasted yellow pepper. Place a portion of the tuna mixture on top of each half. Add some finely chopped fresh basil over this and serve.

Note: This is an elegant introduction to a good dinner and it can also be served as a Sunday or festive brunch.

Peppers

Peppers with Pasta

6 SERVINGS

2 red peppers

2 yellow peppers

2 green peppers

1 onion, peeled

2 garlic cloves, minced

8 tablespoons virgin olive oil

1 pound tagliatelle pasta

small branches of fresh marjoram and
fresh thyme

salt and pepper to taste

1 8-ounce package goat cheese as garnish
(optional) (see Note)

1. Slice the peppers in half and place with the peeled onion under the broiler for about 10–12 minutes until they are well grilled but not burnt. Remove the peppers and onion and allow them to cool.

2. Once they have cooled, carefully remove the skin from the peppers and then slice them into long, thin pieces, about the same length as the tagliatelle. Carefully slice the onion in circles, or at least in lengthy pieces. Place the sliced peppers, onion, minced garlic, and 6 tablespoons of olive oil in an ovenproof bowl. Cover the bowl and keep the mixture warm in the oven at 200°.

3. Boil the pasta in salted water for 6–7 minutes, watching that it remains al dente. Drain the pasta and place it in a serving bowl. Add the peppers and onion from the oven, 2 more tablespoons of olive oil, the marjoram, thyme, and salt, and pepper to taste. Mix all the ingredients well and serve.

Note: This dish may be served hot or lukewarm, but never cold. It is also served without the customary grated cheese on top although you may sprinkle warm or crumbled goat cheese on top of each serving as garnish.

Fresh from a
Monastery Garden

Potatoes

(solanum tuberosum)

Of all vegetables, if one were to ask the question, "Which one is the most popular," I think most people would respond: the potato. The appeal of the potato seems to be universal. Potatoes are found today in outdoor markets and supermarkets all year round, in nearly every part of the world.

The origins of the potato can be traced to the mountains of the Andes. It was first discovered in Peru by the Spanish conquerors around 1532. The following year, a certain Pedro C. de Leon mentions in his *Peru Chronicles*, published in Seville, Spain, that the potatoes, or "papas" as they were called by the native Peruvians, together with corn were considered the essentials in the daily diet of the local Incas. In Europe, the first potatoes were introduced naturally in Spain around 1533. From Spain, its cultivation extended rapidly to France and Italy. By the beginning of the seventeenth century, the potato was already well established in France, where a scientific description of it is offered in the book *A History of Plants (Histoire des Plantes)*, published in 1601. From France, the cultivation of the potato was extended to Germany, Austria, Switzerland, and other countries to the north. In the eighteenth century, a renewed interest was shown in the potato, thanks to the French pharmacist Antoine A. Parmentier, who took it as a cause to spread the knowledge of the potato and its cultivation to every province of France. Parmentier appealed to the King himself, saying that the potato was perhaps the most practical type of food to grow to relieve the King's subjects during times of famine. The appreciation of the potato in France owes so much to Parmentier that even today many of the potato dishes are called in French by the name Parmentier.

Today, more than a hundred varieties of potatoes are known and cultivated around the world. I have a farmer friend here in Millbrook, New York, who specializes in the cultivation of potatoes, and alone raises 28 different varieties. In our own monastic garden, our needs call for the cultivation of 3 or 4 different varieties. Furthermore, we are always able to supply enough for our needs. I particularly appreciate small potatoes, red or otherwise, which enhance many of our culinary dishes.

Potatoes

The potato has a strong nutritional value, as well as being rich in vitamins B_1, B_2, and C. When preparing the potato for cooking, one must take into consideration the nutritional value of its skin. Very often, we peel and discard the skin of the potato when indeed 40 percent of its vitamin C is concentrated there. New potatoes with tender skin might be better served by a thorough washing of the outside prior to use.

Fresh from a
Monastery Garden

Potato Salad Southern French Style

1½ pounds boiling potatoes, cooked and
    peeled

6 eggs, hard-boiled, peeled and chopped

6 small ripe tomatoes, cored and
    quartered

1 small red onion, sliced

½ cup pitted black olives, sliced in half

5 tablespoons capers

VINAIGRETTE

⅓ cup olive oil (more if needed)

4 tablespoons tarragon vinegar (more if
    needed)

1 tablespoon Dijon mustard

salt and freshly ground black pepper
    to taste

1. Cut the potatoes into dice size and place them in a good-size salad bowl. Add the chopped hard-boiled eggs, quartered tomatoes, sliced onion, olives, and capers.

2. Prepare the vinaigrette by combining all the ingredients well. You may add more oil and/or vinegar as needed. Just before serving, pour the vinaigrette dressing over the vegetables. Toss gently and see that the vegetables are well coated. Check the seasonings and serve.

Note: This is an excellent salad to serve during a friendly lunch or brunch.

Potatoes

Potato and Stilton Cheese Soup

6 SERVINGS

4 medium-size potatoes, peeled and cubed

2 leeks (white parts only), finely chopped
(or 1 medium-size onion, chopped)

3 cups water

3 cups low-fat milk

3 tablespoons butter or margarine

3 tablespoons flour

6 sprigs parsley, chopped and minced

salt and white pepper to taste

²/₃ cup crumbled Stilton cheese

1. In a good-size soup kettle, place the potatoes and the leeks (or onion). Pour in the water. Bring to a boil and then reduce the heat to low. Cover the kettle and simmer for about 20 minutes until the potatoes are tender. Turn off the heat and mash the vegetables with the help of a hand masher.

2. Into a separate saucepan, pour the milk and add the butter, flour, parsley, and salt and pepper to taste. Cook the milk mixture over medium heat and stir continually until the milk begins to boil. Pour the milk mixture into the kettle containing the potatoes and cook over medium heat until the soup becomes thick and bubbly. Stir frequently. Check the seasonings.

3. While the soup is hot and bubbly, add the cheese and stir constantly until it melts and blends well with the soup. Serve the soup hot.

Small Potatoes in Yogurt Sauce

6 SERVINGS

$^1/_3$ cup sesame oil (more if needed)

$1^1/_2$ pounds small potatoes (new if possible), peeled

1 16-ounce container plain yogurt

salt and pepper to taste

1 teaspoon cumin

$^1/_2$ cup finely chopped cilantro

5 garlic cloves, chopped and minced

2 medium-size onions, chopped

finely chopped fresh cilantro as garnish

1. Pour the oil into a large skillet or casserole. Add the peeled potatoes (whole) and sauté them gently over medium-low heat for about 5 minutes. Stir frequently and add more oil if needed.

2. Thoroughly butter a deep ovenproof dish with a lid (or a heavy ovenproof pot like Le Creuset with a lid). Place the potatoes into the dish or heavy pot and add the yogurt, salt and pepper, cumin, cilantro, garlic, and onions and mix all the ingredients well. Cover the dish or pot and place it in a preheated oven at 350°. Cook for 50–60 minutes. Garnish the top with finely chopped cilantro. Serve the potatoes hot as an accompaniment to the main course.

Potato Croquettes Belgium Style

6 SERVINGS

1 pound medium-size potatoes, peeled and
   quartered

1/4 cup regular white flour

3 eggs (separate the yolks and the whites)

4 tablespoons heavy cream

4 tablespoons finely grated cheese
   (Parmesan or Gruyère)

ground nutmeg to taste

a pinch of white pepper

oil or butter for frying

1. Boil the potatoes in salted water. When the potatoes are cooked, drain them completely and allow them to dry for at least 1/2 hour in a large deep bowl.

2. Mash the potatoes thoroughly until they turn almost into a puree, but of a rough consistency. Add the flour, well-beaten egg yolks, cream, grated cheese, nutmeg, and white pepper. Mix all the ingredients well. Beat the egg whites well and then incorporate them gradually into the potato mixture. Place the bowl in the refrigerator for an hour.

3. With the help of your two hands, prepare the croquettes by rolling a small amount of the potato mixture back and forth, shaping it into small balls. Place them apart in a flat dish so they do not touch.

4. Pour the oil into a frying pan and over medium heat brown the croquettes on all sides until they are equally coated. Remove them carefully and place them in an ovenproof dish. It is better to fry or brown only a few croquettes at a time. This is delicate work. When they are all done, place the dish in a 200° oven to keep the croquettes warm until you are ready to serve them.

Note: The croquettes are wonderful accompaniments to fish, meat, or egg dishes.

Fresh from a
Monastery Garden

New Potatoes with Sage and Garlic

15 medium-size potatoes, peeled and
   sliced in half

2 onions, sliced

olive oil, as needed

salt to taste

a bunch of fresh sage leaves

6 garlic cloves (fresh if possible)

paprika to taste

$^1/_2$ cup water or milk

1. Bring the potatoes to a boil in a large casserole. When the potatoes are cooked, drain them and set them aside.

2. Pour the oil into a deep skillet, and sauté the onions for about 2 or 3 minutes, stirring often. Add the potatoes and sprinkle them with salt to taste. Stir again and cook thus for 2 or 3 minutes over medium-low heat. Make sure that the potatoes are coated on all sides. (Add more oil if necessary.)

3. Mince the sage leaves and garlic in a food processor and add them to the potatoes. Also add the paprika and continue sautéing and stirring for another minute or two.

4. Thoroughly butter an ovenproof dish with a cover. Place the potatoes in it, pour $^1/_2$ cup of water or milk over them, and cover the pot, placing it in a 350° oven for about 30 minutes. Serve them hot.

Note: This dish is good accompanying a fish, egg, or meat main course.

Potato Salad Pot-au-Feu

8 potatoes, peeled

4 carrots

1 red onion, sliced

8 fresh mushrooms, washed and sliced

finely chopped fresh parsley as garnish

chopped pitted black olives as garnish

VINAIGRETTE

8 tablespoons virgin olive oil

4 tablespoons wine vinegar

1 garlic clove, minced

salt and pepper to taste

1. Boil the potatoes and the carrots until they are tender. Allow them to cool. Cut the potatoes into chunks and slice the carrots. Place them in a salad bowl.

2. Add the sliced onion and the mushrooms and toss gently.

3. Prepare the vinaigrette by mixing all the ingredients well. When you are ready to serve, pour the vinaigrette over the vegetables and toss again until they are well coated. Serve on individual plates and top each portion with some finely chopped parsley and chopped olives as garnish.

Fresh from a
Monastery Garden

Baked Sweet Potatoes

4 SERVINGS

4 good-sized sweet potatoes, washed and
    cleaned

$^3/_4$ cup low-fat sour cream

$^1/_3$ cup maple syrup

$^1/_2$ tablespoon powdered ginger

$^1/_2$ tablespoon nutmeg

salt and pepper to taste

butter

1. Preheat the oven to 400°. Slice each potato carefully in perfect halves and bake them for about 40 to 50 minutes until they are tender. Remove them from the oven and lower it to 350°.

2. With a spoon carefully scoop out the pulp or insides of the potatoes and put the pulp into a large bowl. Make sure the skins of the sweet potatoes remain intact. Mash the pulp with the help of a masher; add the sour cream, maple syrup, ginger, nutmeg, and salt and pepper, and mix this well.

3. Fill the sweet potato shells evenly with the pulp mixture. Put the potatoes in a buttered flat baking dish, and dot each half with a bit of butter. Place them in the oven and bake for about 25–30 minutes. (The potatoes are done when they turn brown on the top.)

Note: This is a delightful and appetizing accompaniment to meat, fish, or egg dishes, especially during the fall or winter.

Potatoes

Sweet Potatoes with Rum

2 pounds sweet potatoes

$^{1}/_{2}$ cup maple syrup

$^{1}/_{2}$ cup orange juice

$^{1}/_{3}$ cup raisins

$^{1}/_{2}$ tablespoon nutmeg

3 tablespoons butter

4 tablespoons rum

a pinch of salt

1. Boil the sweet potatoes for about 15 to 20 minutes. Drain and allow them to cool. Carefully remove their skins.

2. Slice the sweet potatoes lengthwise and carefully place the slices in a buttered flat ovenproof dish.

3. Mix the remaining ingredients in a casserole and cook over low heat for a few minutes, stirring continually. Remove it from the heat before it starts to boil. Pour this mixture in an even fashion over the sweet potatoes. Bake at 350° for about 30–35 minutes, until most of the liquid part turns into a thick sauce or evaporates. Serve hot.

Radishes

(raphanus sativus)

$\mathcal{R}$esearch tells us that the ancient Egyptians cultivated the radish, giving it the name "moon." It was also known to the Mesopotamians and in various regions of the Near East. From these countries, it progressively reached the lands of Greece and Italy. In Greece, the radish was cultivated for both culinary and medicinal purposes, for the Greeks believed the radish to have curative powers against the cough and hemorrhages.

The radish is a vegetable that most gardeners simply adore. It grows in any type of soil, poor or rich, and it can be harvested for consumption in 30 days! No other vegetable has ever demonstrated such a quick growing record! The secret, of course, consists in having consecutive plantings every two weeks, more or less, to assure a prolonged harvest.

The radish is rich in vitamins B and C, but has little other nutritional value as a vegetable. Here in the United States, it is mainly used in salads and as an hors d'oeuvre; however, I have included some recipes to show that the radish is also excellent as a cooked vegetable. All one needs to do is simply experiment with it.

Radishes

Candied Radishes

4 SERVINGS

32 radishes (8 per person)

4 teaspoons butter

3 tablespoons sugar

salt and freshly ground pepper to taste

2 tablespoons water

finely chopped chervil as garnish

1. Choose fresh good-looking radishes, more or less of the same size. Wash them well and trim on both sides.

2. Melt the butter in a deep frying pan, add the sugar, salt and pepper, and 2 tablespoons water. Stir a few times, cover the pan, and cook the radishes over low heat for about 12–15 minutes, or until all the water evaporates. Use the finely chopped chervil to garnish the top of the radishes. Serve the radishes hot as an accompaniment to a main dish (fish, meat, etc.).

Fresh from a
Monastery Garden

Sautéed Radishes

1 pound large radishes, sliced

3 medium-size cucumbers, peeled,
   quartered, and cut into 1-inch pieces

4 tablespoons white or cider vinegar

4 tablespoons oil or butter or margarine

2 tablespoons lemon juice

chopped fresh dill as garnish

1. Place the radishes and the cucumbers in a deep bowl. Sprinkle the vinegar over the vegetables and allow them to stand for $^1/_2$ hour. Then drain the vegetables.

2. Pour the oil or melt the butter in a good-size skillet. Add the vegetables and sauté them gently for 5–6 minutes over medium-low heat. Don't overcook, for the vegetables must remain firm and crisp.

3. When the vegetables are done, sprinkle the lemon juice over them. Mix gently, garnish the top with the chopped dill, and serve warm.

215

Radishes

Radish Greens Pesto Sauce

2 cups chopped fresh radish greens (tops)

1 cup chopped basil leaves

1 cup virgin olive oil

6 garlic cloves, minced

1/2 cup grated Parmesan or Romano cheese

2 tablespoons pignoli nuts (optional)

salt and freshly ground pepper to taste

1. Place the chopped radish greens and the chopped basil leaves in the food processor. (If you don't have one, do it by hand with a mortar and pestle, adding gradually all the ingredients.) Blend at high speed for a few seconds and then stop. Using a spatula, redistribute evenly the greens inside the food processor.

2. Add the olive oil, minced garlic, cheese, nuts, salt, and some freshly ground pepper—blend again at high speed for a few more seconds, until all the ingredients are evenly blended and mixed.

Note: Use this delicious sauce with pasta dishes, and also with certain vegetables like tomatoes and potatoes. It can also be used with fish and eggs. The sauce can be stored in the refrigerator for a long time.

Radish Canapés

20 medium-size fresh radishes, washed, ends trimmed, cut in halves, and then thinly sliced

2 ripe avocados

1 shallot, chopped and minced

3 tablespoons olive oil

4 tablespoons fresh lemon juice

salt and pepper to taste

finely chopped fresh cilantro

6–8 slices bread and/or crackers or tortillas

1. Whenever possible, use radishes grown in your own garden.

2. Peel the avocados and puree them with the help of a good fork. Add the shallot, oil, lemon juice, salt and pepper, and chopped cilantro and mix well. Add the sliced radishes and again mix thoroughly until the mixture becomes smooth and even.

3. Toast the bread slices and afterward cut each slice in 4 equal pieces. Spread the radish-avocado mixture on each and serve to your guests. If you do not wish to use bread, use your favorite kind of cracker or tortilla.

Note: This radish-avocado mixture can be prepared ahead of time and kept in the refrigerator until you are ready to use it.

Salad Greens

In early summer, a variety of salad greens begins to arrive in our monastery garden. With subsequent plantings throughout the season, we are happy to enjoy the freshness and delight that the combination of these greens brings to the table for a long time. All the cook has to do is to use his or her imagination to create marvelous concoctions with the diverse variety of tastes, texture, flavors, and nuances of colors placed at his or her disposal. Among the greens cultivated and served at the monastic table are the following:

LETTUCE
(*Lactuca sativa*)

Lettuce is perhaps the best known and the most cultivated among the salad greens. It was already known in antiquity, where the ancient Egyptians considered it a sacred vegetable. They used it in ritual ceremonies as a form of offering and homage to the goddess of fertility, for they strongly believed that lettuce possessed aphrodisiac-like qualities. The Greeks and the Romans found other virtues and medicinal qualities in lettuce. For instance, they strongly recommended the consumption of lettuce by insomniacs, for they considered it a great help to sleep.

Today there are hundreds and hundreds of varieties of lettuce available for home cultivation in the garden. There is also a great variety available at the supermarkets. Thank God, gone by are the days when iceberg was the only type of lettuce found in the supermarkets of America. Among the favorites in our gardens are Bibb, Boston lettuce, romaine, Batavia, and those whose seeds we bring from France: Lollo Rossa and Merveille des Quatre Saisons.

CHICORY
(*Cichorium endivia*)

This type of chicory, sometimes called endive in the supermarkets (not to be confused with Belgium endive, see page 115) has a bit of a bitter flavor, and when mixed with other greens in a salad bowl it creates a marvelous contrast. Our favorite type is the one called in French *chicorée frisée*. Among this type of frisée, the

Salad Greens

one that renders excellent results for us, is the *grosse pancalière*, whose seeds we obtain from France but they can probably also be found here. One of the many attributes of the frisée, besides its exquisite taste and texture, is the fact that it is also not heat and cold sensitive. It lingers in the garden long after the first frost.

ARUGULA
(Eruca vesicaria)

The arugula is sometimes called rocket, from the French *roquette*. It is a plant that had its origin in the Mediterranean countries of Europe, where it is still widely cultivated and greatly appreciated in salads. Its peppery flavor blends harmoniously with some of the milder greens in the salad bowl. We cultivate two or three types of arugula in our garden: the annual, which is the one easily available in American gardens, then a French type called *Roquette cultivée*. And we are particularly fond of the *Arugula salvatica*, which is a perennial. The seeds from this last one were brought to us from Venice, Italy, by a dear friend who visited there. It has remained a perennial in our garden, where it grows so profusely that each year we have to discard some of its many plants for it tends to take over the garden. Friends and neighbors in Dutchess County, New York, have benefited from it, and now it has become abundant in their own gardens as well.

OTHER SALAD GREENS

There are other salad greens that we also cultivate in our garden, with obviously wonderful results for the salad bowl because they complement each other. These are escarole, mâche, mesclun, mustard greens, and radishes. I am particularly fond of watercress, and use it frequently in our salads and other dishes like soups, but unfortunately we don't possess the necessary conditions for its cultivation on our property. (Watercress grows well by streams, as its name tells us, and we have none on the monastery land.)

Boston Lettuce Mimosa Salad

4 SERVINGS

1 medium-size head of Boston lettuce

1 medium-size cucumber, peeled and sliced

1 medium-size onion, sliced

2 hard-boiled eggs, finely chopped

VINAIGRETTE

6 tablespoons virgin olive oil

3 tablespoons balsamic vinegar

1 teaspoon French mustard

salt and pepper to taste

1. Wash the lettuce thoroughly and drain it. Separate the individual leaves and place them in a bowl. Add the sliced cucumber and onion.

2. Prepare a simple vinaigrette by mixing the ingredients well. When you are ready to serve, pour the vinaigrette over the salad and toss it lightly.

3. Serve the salad on four individual plates and sprinkle over each serving the finely chopped boiled eggs.

Note: This is an easy and excellent salad to serve all year round.

Salad Greens

Escarole Salad with Hard-Boiled Eggs

(SALADE DE FRISÉE)

6 SERVINGS

1 head of tender escarole

1 red onion, thinly sliced

24 cherry tomatoes (4 per person)

6 hard-boiled eggs, sliced in halves, lengthwise

VINAIGRETTE

8 tablespoons virgin olive oil

1 tablespoon lemon juice

3 tablespoons balsamic vinegar

salt and freshly ground pepper to taste

1. Wash and clean the escarole well. Choose the best and most tender leaves from the center. Discard the tougher ones from the outer part. Drain them thoroughly and mix them with the thinly sliced onion. Distribute the escarole and onion mixture evenly among six serving plates.

2. Wash and dry the cherry tomatoes. Slice them in halves. Evenly distribute the eggs and tomatoes among the six plates. Place them on the top of the escarole in a decorative fashion.

3. Just before serving, prepare the vinaigrette. Mix the ingredients well and pour some of the dressing over each salad serving.

Note: This delicious salad can be served as an appetizer or as a separate dish after the main course. It is particularly appetizing during the summer months when you are able to harvest the vegetables from your own garden.

Fresh from a
Monastery Garden

Romaine Lettuce Salad alla Romana

1 head of romaine lettuce, washed, dried, and cut into bite-size pieces

6 medium-size well-ripened tomatoes, quartered

1 red onion, thinly sliced into rings

1 cup pitted green olives

2 cups cubed fresh mozzarella cheese

VINAIGRETTE

8 tablespoons virgin olive oil (more if necessary)

2 tablespoons red wine vinegar (more if necessary)

2 tablespoons lemon juice (more if necessary)

salt and black pepper to taste

1. Set the salad plates on your kitchen table and distribute the lettuce evenly among all the plates.

2. Place the tomatoes, onion, and olives in a deep bowl. Mix and toss gently. Then distribute them evenly over the beds of romaine lettuce on the plates. Garnish each serving with the cubed mozzarella cheese.

3. When you are ready to serve, prepare and mix the vinaigrette ingredients well. Pour even amounts over each serving. Serve right away.

Note: This dish is a wonderful introduction to a good meal, either lunch, brunch, or supper.

Salad Greens

Arugula Gourmet Salad

4–6 SERVINGS

VINAIGRETTE

⅓ cup fruity olive oil (extra-virgin if possible)

3 tablespoons balsamic vinegar or a good red wine vinegar

salt and freshly ground pepper to taste

SALAD

1 large bunch of fresh arugula, washed and trimmed

1 head of radicchio, leaves sliced lengthwise in half

2 Belgium endives, leaves sliced lengthwise in half

1 small bunch of watercress, stems trimmed

½ pound mâche, washed and drained

1. Prepare the vinaigrette. Mix all the ingredients well.

2. Just before serving, place the salad ingredients in a large salad bowl, pouring the previously prepared vinaigrette over it. Toss and see that all the greens are well coated with the dressing. Serve immediately.

Fresh from a
Monastery Garden

Basic Mâche Salad

1 large bunch of mâche; wash and keep
   the leaves whole

2 Belgium endives

1 small onion

2 apples

finely chopped fresh parsley or chives as
   garnish (optional)

DRESSING

½ cup low-fat plain yogurt or sour cream

1 tablespoon crème fraîche

2 tablespoons olive oil

2 tablespoons fresh lemon juice

1 teaspoon creamy mustard

salt and pepper to taste

1. Wash and dry the rest of the vegetables well. Slice them (peel the apples first) and place them in a large salad bowl with the mâche. Add the sliced apples. Mix gently.

2. Prepare the dressing by mixing all the ingredients well in a separate bowl. Beat steadily until the mixture turns into an even and creamy dressing. (Refrigerate it until you are ready to use.)

3. Just before serving, pour the dressing over the salad. Toss the salad and serve it right away. This salad can be garnished with finely chopped parsley or chives on top of each serving.

227

Salad Greens

Romaine Lettuce Salad with Gorgonzola Cheese

6—8 SERVINGS

1 head of romaine lettuce, cut into
   3-inch sections

1 small head of radicchio, thinly sliced

1 red onion, thinly sliced

1 small cucumber, peeled and thinly sliced

1 8-ounce container sour cream, low-fat is
   fine

$^3/_4$ cup Gorgonzola cheese, crumbled

2 tablespoons virgin olive oil

4 tablespoons fresh lemon juice

salt and pepper to taste

1. Place the vegetables in a good-size salad bowl.

2. In a separate bowl, mix the sour cream, cheese, olive oil, lemon juice, salt, and pepper. Beat by hand until all the ingredients are well mixed and turn into a creamy dressing.

3. Just before serving, pour the creamy dressing over the vegetables and gently toss the salad. Serve immediately after.

Note: This is an easy salad to prepare and it can be served all year round.

Romaine Lettuce Soup

6 SERVINGS

1 head of romaine lettuce, washed and sliced

2 leeks, including the green parts, washed and sliced

3 medium-size potatoes, peeled and diced

8½ cups water

2 garlic cloves, peeled and minced

salt and pepper to taste

1 8-ounce container heavy cream

croutons as garnish (for hot soup)

1. Place the sliced and diced vegetables in a soup pot. Add the water and the garlic, and bring the liquid to a boil. Lower the heat to medium-low and continue cooking for another 20–25 minutes. Remove the soup from the heat and allow it to cool.

2. Whirl the soup in a food processor or in a blender. Reheat it over low heat, add the seasonings and the heavy cream, and stir continually until all ingredients are evenly mixed. This soup can be served hot or cold. If served hot, add some croutons to each serving as garnish.

Salad Greens

Arugula Pesto Sauce

MAKES 1 CUP

6 garlic cloves, minced

1 large bunch of arugula leaves, chopped

¹/₃ cup well-chopped pignoli nuts
  (pine nuts)

6 teaspoons grated Romano cheese
  (or Parmesan)

1 cup virgin olive oil

a pinch of salt and pepper

Place all the ingredients in a food processor or blender and mix thoroughly for a few minutes until everything is well blended.

Note: Use this sauce for pasta dishes and also with certain vegetables like tomatoes and zucchinis. It can be also used to stuff hard-boiled eggs.

Fresh from a
Monastery Garden

Basic Arugula Salad

1 large bunch of arugula, washed and
  trimmed

1 small head of radicchio, sliced

1 small cucumber, peeled and thinly sliced

1 small onion, sliced

crumbled blue cheese (or goat cheese) to
  taste as garnish

VINAIGRETTE

6 tablespoons virgin olive oil

3 tablespoons tarragon-scented vinegar

salt and pepper to taste

1. Place the arugula, radicchio, cucumber, and onion in a good-sized bowl.

2. When you are ready to serve, prepare the vinaigrette by mixing all the ingredients well. Pour the vinaigrette over the vegetables. Toss the salad lightly and see that the vegetables are well coated with the vinaigrette. Serve on individual dishes, and place some crumbled blue cheese on top of each serving as garnish.

Note: This salad is ideal for serving after the main course and before dessert.

Salad Greens

Creamy Watercress Soup
(POTAGE CRESONNIÈRE)

4 SERVINGS

3 large potatoes, peeled and sliced

2 leeks, sliced (white part only)

1 large bunch of watercress, chopped

7 cups water (more if needed)

3 tablespoons butter

1 cup heavy cream or half and half or
   plain milk or low-fat milk

salt and freshly ground pepper to taste

1. Place the potatoes, leeks, and watercress in a large saucepan. Add the water and bring to a boil. Cover the pot and simmer the soup gently for 30 minutes. Set the saucepan aside and allow the soup to cool.

2. When the soup has cooled, blend it in small batches in the blender.

3. Melt the butter in the saucepan and add the batches of blended soup as they come out of the blender. At the end, add the cream and salt and pepper. Stir and mix the soup well. Over medium-low heat, bring the soup to a light boil. Stir again and cover the saucepan. Serve the soup hot or refrigerate for a few hours and serve it cold.

Note: This is a delicious and elegant first course for a good dinner.

Fresh from a
Monastery Garden

Spinach, Swiss Chard, Sorrel

(rumex acetosa)

$\mathcal{G}$reen leaf vegetables that are usually eaten cooked are listed here in contrast to the green leaf vegetables that are eaten raw, usually in salads. Spinach is generally the exception to the rule, since it can be eaten both ways.

SPINACH
(Spinacia oleracea)

$\mathcal{S}$pinach has gone through different periods of evolution and change throughout the centuries. The original plant seems to have been the *Spinacia letandra,* which grew wild throughout Asia Minor. From there, spinach was imported to Europe and other parts of the world, undergoing some changes in the process of adaptation to new territories and forms of cultivation. The Europeans first discovered spinach in the Middle Ages, around the time of the Crusades, and were happy to bring home the first seeds for cultivation. Later on, during the time of the Arab invasions of Southern Europe, spinach saw further expansion of its cultivation throughout the continents. It is claimed by some that the original Arabic name for spinach was *esbanach,* which was then latinized *spinacia* in Europe. During the eleventh century, Seville in Spain became one of the great centers of its cultivation for spinach that was not only used for culinary purposes but also for medicinal ones. During the Renaissance, Catherine de' Medici and her Italian culinary entourage did much to enhance the value of spinach at the table in Paris and throughout France.

Spinach is rich in vitamins A, B, and C as well as in iron and other minerals. This is why it has become appropriately so integral a part of our contemporary twentieth-century diet almost everywhere on the globe. Its cultivation in the garden is relatively easy except for the fact that it does not like extremely hot temperatures. For this reason, in our monastery garden, spinach is usually cultivated in early spring and late summer for a fall harvest. Spinach does well in cool weather, and one of the great pleasures of late spring and early summer is the arrival of new tender spinach at the monastic table.

Spinach,
Swiss Chard, Sorrel

Swiss Chard

(Beta vulgaris cicla)

Swiss chard plays an integral part in all Latin Mediterranean cooking. Italy, France, and Spain are probably where the largest concentration of world cultivation of Swiss chard takes place. The origins of Swiss chard seem to have been both the borders of the Mediterranean Sea and the Atlantic Ocean. The ancient Greeks and the Romans appreciated the use of chard at the table, especially the poor people of those days who often used it in soups and other dishes. Swiss chard and beets belong to the same type of family, with the difference that the beet develops an edible root. Both greens are excellent when cooked and they often substitute for spinach at the monastery table, especially during the height of summer when our spinach plants go to seed. I always had a certain preference for Swiss chards. It probably has to do with some of my own childhood memories. Swiss chard was frequently used at home and in many cases was preferred to spinach. I usually cook the green leaves as I would spinach and save the stems and cook them separately. There are different types of chards for garden cultivation. We plant two or three different varieties in our own garden: regular Swiss chard, available just about everywhere in this country, the *poirée blonde,* whose seeds we bring from France and which produces a much larger sort of chard. And last, but not least, we also plant some years the red type of chard, which is both edible and at the same time ornamental in the garden. One of the great qualities of Swiss chard is the fact that it is resistant to both heat and cold at the same time. It does well during the heat of summer and tends to endure the first frosts, surviving well into late fall and early winter.

Sorrel

(Rumex acetosa)

Although not yet as well known in the United States as it is in Europe, sorrel is beginning, however, to receive more and more recognition among American gardeners and chefs. Perhaps the day will come soon when it will be easily available in the supermarkets. Those who have it in their garden do not have to worry about it, for sorrel is a perennial that returns every year and tends to appear in the garden

Fresh from a Monastery Garden

before any other vegetable. Early in the spring when one longs for something fresh from the garden, although it is still too early to harvest much of anything, I always make recourse to the one thing that is available at that time, sorrel. Unfailingly, it is there before anything else and one can prepare wonderful soups and delightful sauces with it.

Spinach,
Swiss Chard, Sorrel

Spinach Chiffonnade

4–6 SERVINGS

12 porcini mushrooms (6–8 portobello
   mushrooms can be substituted)

6 tablespoons olive oil

1 pound fresh spinach (young ones if possible)

4 teaspoons butter (or substitute)

4 tablespoons lemon juice

salt and pepper to taste

SHALLOT SAUCE (BEURRE À L'ÍCHALOTE)

2 shallots, finely chopped

1 cup dry white wine

5 teaspoons butter (or equal substitute)

10 tablespoons water

salt and freshly ground pepper

lemon juice

1. To prepare the mushrooms, first of all, soak them in water for $1/2$ hour, then wash and rinse them carefully, so that all sand or extra dirt is removed. Chop them roughly. Pour some olive oil (about 5 tablespoons) in a large frying pan and sauté the mushrooms over medium heat for a few minutes until they become tender. Remove them from the heat and set them aside.

2. Wash and rinse the spinach and drain. Pour the remaining (1 tablespoon) oil in a large casserole, add the butter, spinach, lemon juice, salt, and pepper and cook the spinach over medium heat for 4–5 minutes, stirring constantly. Remove from the heat.

3. Place the lightly cooked spinach in a good-size, well-buttered, ovenproof dish. Spread evenly over the spinach the previously cooked mushrooms. Cover the dish with aluminum foil and place it in the oven at 150° while preparing the Shallot Sauce.

4. To make the Shallot Sauce, place the finely chopped shallots in a small-size pan and add $1/2$ cup of wine. Cook over medium-low heat, stirring continually, until the wine is almost completely evaporated. Add the butter, water, the rest of the wine, salt, and pepper and continue stirring for about 3 minutes until the sauce is done.

5. Remove the spinach dish from the oven, spread the shallot sauce evenly over the whole dish. Sprinkle some extra lemon juice on the top. Cover with aluminum foil and place the dish in the oven at 300°. Cook for 20–25 minutes. Serve hot.

Spinach Terrine

(Terrine des épinards)

4 servings

1 pound fresh spinach

1 onion, chopped

2 tablespoons butter

Béchamel Sauce

2 tablespoons butter

2 tablespoons cornstarch

2 cups milk

a pinch of nutmeg

salt and pepper to taste

4 eggs

1. Wash and drain the spinach. Chop it coarsely. Boil it for 2 minutes in salted water and then drain thoroughly. Set aside.

2. Sauté the chopped onion in the butter until it begins to turn golden. Withdraw from the heat and mix it with the spinach.

3. Prepare the Béchamel Sauce by melting the butter in a saucepan over medium-low heat, adding the cornstarch, and stirring continuously with a whisk or wooden spoon. Add the milk gradually, whisking or stirring continuously. Add the nutmeg and salt and pepper and continue stirring. When the sauce begins to boil, reduce the heat and continue cooking slowly until it thickens. Set it aside.

4. In a large, deep bowl beat the eggs well, add the Béchamel Sauce, and mix. Add the spinach-onion mixture and mix all the ingredients thoroughly.

5. Butter a bread pan or mold well. Pour the spinach mixture into it. Place the bread in a 350° oven within a long, flat container with water. (This dish is cooked in what is called the bain-marie.) The water should reach about halfway up the bread pan. Cook for 30 minutes, and then wait until it cools a bit before unmolding it. This dish can be served hot or cold.

Note: Swiss chard may be substituted for the spinach.

Spinach,
Swiss Chard, Sorrel

Spinach with Croutons

2 pounds fresh spinach, washed and trimmed

$^{1}/_{2}$ cup heavy cream or half and half

3 hard-boiled eggs, chopped, as garnish

BÉCHAMEL SAUCE

2 tablespoons butter

1 tablespoon cornstarch

1 cup milk

1 tablespoon dry vermouth

salt and pepper to taste

a pinch of nutmeg

CROUTONS

6 slices of bread

6 tablespoons olive oil

2 garlic cloves, chopped and minced

a dash of dried thyme

1. Cook the spinach in salted boiling water for the space of about 8 minutes. Drain and run cold water over it to help retain the fresh color. Drain the spinach thoroughly for a second time and then chop. Set aside.

2. Prepare the Béchamel by melting 2 tablespoons of butter in a stainless steel pot over medium-low heat. Add 1 tablespoon of cornstarch and stir continually with a wooden spoon. Add little by little, 1 cup of milk while stirring continuously. Add 1 tablespoon dry vermouth, the salt and pepper to taste, and a pinch of nutmeg. When the sauce begins to boil, reduce the heat and continue cooking and stirring until it thickens. When it is done, set aside.

3. Prepare the croutons by cutting 6 slices of bread into even cubes. Pour 6 tablespoons of olive oil into a wide skillet, add the 2 garlic cloves, chopped and minced, bread cubes, and a dash of dried thyme over the cubes, and mix the ingredients well. Then sauté over low heat for 3–5 minutes, while stirring continually. When the cubes are browned on all sides remove them from the heat and set aside.

4. Butter thoroughly a long, ovenproof dish and place in it the cooked spinach, Béchamel, heavy cream, and croutons. Mix all the ingredients well and see that they are evenly distributed throughout the dish. Place the dish in a preheated oven at 300° for about 20–25 minutes. Serve the dish hot and garnish each serving with a spoonful or two of hard-boiled eggs on top.

Spinach,
Swiss Chard, Sorrel

Spinach-Stuffed Apples

8 SERVINGS

8 large apples

1 lemon, juiced

1/4 pound fresh (cleaned and washed) or
   frozen spinach

1 small onion, thinly sliced

3 tablespoons, plus 4 teaspoons butter

1.5-ounce box of raisins

salt and pepper to taste

1. Wash and clean the apples well. Using a thin knife and a teaspoon, carefully scoop out the inner parts of each apple, making sure the shape remains whole.

2. Cut the inner or scooped-out parts of the apples into small pieces and pour the juice from the lemon over them. Mix well.

3. Cut the spinach and the onion into thin, small pieces. Melt 3 tablespoons of butter into a frying pan. And the spinach, onion, raisins, and cut apple pieces; sauté for 10 minutes. Add salt and pepper and mix well. Stir frequently.

4. Fill the apples with the stuffing and put 1/2 teaspoon of butter on the top of each. Place them in an oven at 350° for 20 minutes. Serve them hot.

Fresh from a
Monastery Garden

Swiss Chard and Egg Noodles

1 pound fresh Swiss chard

1 12-ounce package egg noodles

a pinch of salt

6 garlic cloves, peeled

12 basil leaves

4 sprigs Italian parsley

10 tablespoons olive oil to taste

salt and pepper to taste

grated Parmesan cheese

1. Wash and clean well the chards. Remove the stems and chop the leaves. (The stems can be used separately for another dish.) Place the leaves in a large casserole filled with water and bring to a boil. Lower the heat to medium-low and cook for 8–10 minutes. Drain and set aside.

2. In a separate casserole, cook the noodles according to instructions on the package. Add a pinch of salt and drain.

3. While the Swiss chard and the noodles are cooking, place the garlic cloves, basil, and parsley in a food processor and whirl several times until they are finely chopped and minced.

4. Heat the olive oil in a heavy casserole, add the garlic and herbs. Stir continually for about ½ minute. Add the Swiss chard, noodles, and salt and pepper and continue stirring until all the ingredients are well mixed. Serve hot and sprinkle grated cheese on top.

Spinach,
Swiss Chard, Sorrel

Swiss Chard Mont-Voiron

(BLETTES DU MONT-VOIRON)

4 SERVINGS

20 Swiss chard stalks

salt to taste

1/2 stick of butter

1 lemon

2 garlic cloves, minced

6 tablespoons grated cheese

2 eggs, beaten

pepper to taste

1. Separate the green parts of the chards from the stalks. (Keep the greens to use in another form or dish). Slice the stalks approximately 3 inches long. Place them in a casserole with boiling water. Add salt and cook for about 5–6 minutes maximum. Then drain.

2. Melt the butter in a large, heavy skillet. Add the chard stalks, juice from 1 lemon, and minced garlic and cook over medium-low heat for about 3 minutes. Stir frequently. Add the grated cheese and continue stirring for about 2 more minutes so that all the ingredients are well mixed.

3. Just before serving, beat the eggs and add salt and pepper to taste. Add all this to the chard-cheese mixture. Stir and mix well until the eggs are cooked and well blended with all the other ingredients. Serve immediately.

Fresh from a
Monastery Garden

Cold Sorrel Soup

a large bunch of sorrel leaves

1 large leek, white part only

3 tablespoons butter

6 cups water

1 vegetable bouillon cube

1 large cucumber, peeled, seeded, and
    sliced

1 8-ounce container half and half

4 tablespoons lemon juice

salt and pepper to taste

6 thin slices of smoked salmon, as garnish

1. Trim and chop the sorrel. Discard the stems. Wash and slice the leek, discard the green parts.

2. Melt the butter in a soup pot, add the sorrel and leek and cook over medium-low heat for about 2 minutes until the vegetables are wilted and begin to change color. Add the water and the bouillon cube. Bring the soup to a boil, cover the pot, and cook thus for 5 minutes. Then set the soup aside from the heat and let it cool.

3. Place the cucumber slices and half and half in a blender and whirl it for a minute. Add the sorrel soup, lemon juice, and salt and pepper, and whirl some more until all the ingredients are thoroughly mixed and creamy. (This can be done in one or two or three stages, depending on the amount of the soup.) When it is all done, re-frigerate it for a few hours.

4. Just before serving, slice the salmon in thin long slices julienne style to use it as garnish. Serve the soup cold and top it with the salmon slices.

245

Spinach,
Swiss Chard, Sorrel

Sorrel Omelet

(OMELETTE À L'OSEILLE)

2–3 SERVINGS

6 tablespoons butter

1 bunch of sorrel leaves, trimmed,
    stemmed, and chopped

1 8-ounce container heavy cream

6 eggs

salt and pepper to taste

finely chopped chervil as garnish

1. Melt 3 tablespoons of the butter in a large skillet, add the chopped sorrel, and cook for a few minutes until the sorrel turns soft and is thoroughly wilted. Place it in a bowl and add half of the heavy cream. Mix it well.

2. Beat the eggs in a bowl, counting at least 20 brisk strokes. Add the remaining heavy cream and salt and pepper to taste and continue beating the mixture until it all blends.

3. Melt the 3 remaining tablespoons of butter in the skillet, run it all over the pan, and let it get bubbly hot but do not let it burn. Pour in the egg mixture quickly before the butter begins to turn brown. Spread the mixture evenly around the skillet with the help of a spatula. When the egg mixture sets firmly on the bottom, turn the omelet by placing a large dish over it and turning upside down quickly. Gently slide the reverse side of the omelet back into the skillet, pour the sorrel mixture over it, cover the skillet, and allow it to cook for about 2 minutes. Fold one half of the omelet carefully over the other half.

4. Slice the omelet into 2 or 3 even portions and serve immediately after on warm plates. Place some finely chopped chervil on the top of each portion as garnish.

Note: This is a very popular omelet in France and is an attractive dish to serve for a Sunday brunch among close friends.

Fresh from a
Monastery Garden

Sorrel Sauce

¹/₂ pound sorrel leaves

1¹/₂ cups vegetable or fish stock, or
    chicken stock

1¹/₂ tablespoons butter

I tablespoon cornstarch

¹/₃ cup heavy cream

salt and pepper to taste

a dash of nutmeg

1. Wash and trim the sorrel leaves. Discard the stalk in the middle and chop the leaves.

2. Bring the stock to a boil, add the sorrel, and simmer for 6–7 minutes. Set the sorrel aside for a few minutes, allowing it to cool, then put it through a blender.

3. Melt the butter in a saucepan, add the cornstarch, and stir continually until it is evenly blended. Add the blended sorrel, and continue cooking over low heat for 3 or 4 minutes while stirring constantly. Add the heavy cream, salt and pepper to taste, and a dash of nutmeg and continue stirring for a minute or two until the sauce is perfectly blended.

Note: This sauce can be served over white fish, white rice, noodles, and over hard-boiled eggs.

247

Spinach,
Swiss Chard, Sorrel

Squash

(cucurbita)

The squash is a fruit-vegetable of tropical origin. Traces have been found showing that it was already being cultivated in Peru and the Andean countries surrounding it twelve hundred years B.C. There are many species of squash or "cucurbits" that belong to the same family. The most renowned today is the pumpkin, or *potiron* in French, but there are also other commonly used varieties: butternut squash, acorn squash, yellow squash, gourds, Hubbard, etc. We must remember that even the melon belongs to this family—it is simply another variety.

The squash is a rustic, basic plant that usually does not need much care except for a good amount of sun and water. It grows in almost any type of soil, though best results are achieved with a soil rich in compost and of a certain depth. We usually wait to plant our different varieties of squash at least until mid-May. Here in the northeastern United States, we always have to deal with the fact that all it takes is an unseasonably cold night to kill the young tender plants or seedlings. Most members of the squash family are not cold resistant—all to the contrary!

We grow different varieties in our small monastic garden. They provide great help in the kitchen, where we use them not only to serve at the table but also to make jams, preserves, and chutney. The squash is a very resilient fruit-vegetable that if kept under the right conditions and temperature can last for a long time in the cellar, and thus be the source of culinary delights during the long winter months.

I still retain vivid recollections of the old monastic traditions of France. During the time of the harvest, the monks and nuns lined up the squash and pumpkins of all sizes and colors along the cloister corridor for the winter months and the cook would then come occasionally and fetch the ones he needed for the kitchen. I was always amused to see the monks marching in daily processions through a cloister corridor lined with pumpkins. There was a certain resemblance between the line of pumpkins in perfect order and the line of monks in procession.

Squash

Festive Pumpkin Soup

1 medium-size pumpkin, peeled and diced

6 potatoes, peeled and diced

2 leeks, sliced (white parts only)

1 onion, diced

2 garlic cloves, minced

1 celery stalk, finely sliced

12 cups water

salt and pepper to taste

1 egg yolk

1/2 cup heavy cream

grated Gruyère cheese for the table

1. Place the vegetables in a large soup pot. Add 12 cups of water and bring the soup to a boil. Lower the heat to medium, add the salt and pepper, and cook for about 45 minutes without covering the pot.

2. When the soup is done, allow it to cool and then whirl it in the blender. Reheat the soup gradually.

3. Beat the egg yolk in a bowl, add the heavy cream, and continue beating until the ingredients are well mixed. Pour this mixture into the creamy soup and stir for one minute or two until all the elements are perfectly blended. Serve the soup hot accompanied by a bowl of grated Gruyère cheese at the table.

Note: This is a delightful soup to serve when pumpkins and squash are in season.

Fresh from a
Monastery Garden

Pumpkin Squash au Gratin
(GRATIN DE POTIRON)

4—6 SERVINGS

4 pounds fresh pumpkin

1½ cups split orange lentils

salt

1 pint half and half

1 cup thinly sliced low-fat mozzarella
  cheese (in flakes)

freshly ground pepper to taste

½ teaspoon nutmeg

finely grated cheese to taste

1. Peel the pumpkin and slice it into cubes (about 8 to 10 cups). Combine the pumpkin and the lentils in a large saucepan with water. Add salt. Bring the water to a boil, then reduce the heat and continue cooking for another 12–15 minutes, until the lentils are well cooked.

2. Drain the vegetables and place them back in the empty saucepan. Add the half and half, mozzarella cheese, salt and freshly ground pepper to taste, and nutmeg. Mix thoroughly and mash the mixture well with the help of a masher until it turns into a smooth puree.

3. Thoroughly butter a long, flat ovenproof dish and pour the vegetable mixture into it. With the help of a spatula, spread the mixture evenly. Sprinkle finely grated cheese on the top of the mixture.

4. Place the dish in a 350° preheated oven. Cook for about 20 minutes and then serve hot.

Note: This dish is a good accompaniment as a side dish to the main course.

Squash

Acorn Squash Soup

4–6 SERVINGS

6 tablespoons olive oil

2 onions, chopped

8 cups water or vegetable stock (or chicken stock)

3 acorn squash, peeled, halved, seeded, and cut into chunks

1 potato, peeled and cubed

2 carrots, sliced

$^{1}/_{2}$ cup fresh parsley, chopped and finely minced, plus more chopped parsley as garnish

salt and pepper to taste

a pinch of nutmeg

1. Pour the olive oil into a good-size saucepan and sauté the onions over low heat for about 3 minutes. Turn off the heat, add the water or stock, cover the pan, and let the steam from the sautéed onions permeate the water or stock for 15 minutes.

2. Add the chunks of squash, the cubed potato, and the sliced carrots. Stir well and bring the water to a boil. Reduce the heat, add the parsley and seasonings, cover the pot, and allow the soup to simmer for 30–40 minutes. Add more water if necessary.

3. Allow the soup to cool and whirl it in a blender in small batches. Return the pureed soup to a clean pot. Reheat it over low heat, stir well, and serve the soup hot. Garnish with some more parsley on top of each serving.

Fresh from a
Monastery Garden

Acorn Squash Stuffed with Goat Cheese

2 medium-size acorn squash

salt

4 tablespoons olive oil

1 onion, chopped

2 large tomatoes, finely chopped

2 garlic cloves, minced

a handful of fresh parsley, finely chopped

fresh rosemary leaves, if possible

a few fresh basil leaves, finely chopped

1 8-ounce package goat cheese

4 tablespoons bread crumbs

pepper to taste

1. Slice the squash in perfect halves and remove the seeds. Fill a large casserole or saucepan with water, add salt, and bring the water to a boil. Place the squash halves in the casserole, cut side down, and boil for 8 to 10 minutes. Drain them thoroughly.

2. Heat the oil in a large skillet and add the onion, chopped tomatoes, garlic, and herbs. Sauté for a few minutes until the mixture turns into a sauce. Remove the sauce from the heat and pour it into a bowl.

3. Crumble the goat cheese and add it to the sauce. Add the bread crumbs and salt and pepper, and mix all the ingredients well.

4. Butter a flat baking dish and arrange the squash halves on it. Divide the sauce mixture evenly among the squash halves, filling the cavities to the top. Bake in a pre-heated oven at 300° for 30 minutes. Serve hot.

Tomatoes

(lycopersicon esculentum)

The tomato, properly speaking, is not a vegetable but a fruit. Its origin lies in the ancient mountains of Peru, the Andes. The early Spaniards who discovered and settled in that part of the Americas made acquaintance with the tomato there and later on introduced it into Europe. The Spaniards found that the native Indians used the tomato to make a very spicy sauce, which is the origin of our tomato sauce and salsa, so popular today.

The tomato as well as the potato, also recently discovered, began to be cultivated in Europe especially in Italy, where it received the name *pomodore*, that is golden apple. From Italy and Spain, the tomato was introduced into France, where the French began calling it *pomme d'amour*, that is "love apple," because they believed the tomato to have strong aphrodisiac qualities.

Today, the tomato has gained acceptance everywhere and it is cultivated worldwide. It may well be that it is one of the most popularly consumed fruits, especially among those fruits regularly eaten as a vegetable. Today there are endless varieties for cultivation, from those that mature early to those that arrive later in the season and are excellent for canning for winter use. Tomatoes love the sun, and the ones that arrive in August or early September usually taste better, for they have been saturated by the heat from the sun. Tomatoes are rich in vitamins A, B, and C, as well as in iron and magnesium. The one area of the tomato that sometimes certain people find difficult to digest is the skin surrounding the fruit. In that case it is better to peel it before eating. In the monastery we spend a great part of September and October making tomato sauce and canning it for the winter ahead. I usually boil the tomatoes whole for about 2 minutes and then peel them before turning them into a sauce. This process makes the peeling of the tomato simpler and faster.

Tomatoes

Tomato Velouté

4 tablespoons olive oil

I pound fresh tomatoes, peeled and
    seeded

3 carrots, sliced

2 onions, sliced

I potato, peeled and sliced

I 8-ounce can tomato sauce

a few sprigs parsley, finely chopped

$1/4$ teaspoon dried thyme

salt and freshly ground pepper to taste

8 cups water

$1/2$ 8-ounce container crème fraîche or
    low-fat yogurt

1. Pour the oil into a large saucepan and add the tomatoes, carrots, onions, potato, tomato sauce, parsley, thyme, and salt and pepper. Sauté gently over low heat for about 3 minutes while stirring continually.

2. After the 3 minutes, add the water and stir well. Bring the water to a boil and cover the pot. Cook for $1/2$ hour over medium-low heat. Stir from time to time.

3. When the soup is done, set it aside and allow it to cool. Then blend the soup in small batches in a blender. If the soup is to be served cold, place it in the refrigerator. If it is to be served hot, reheat it before serving but do not let it boil again. In either case, just before serving, add the crème fraîche or yogurt and mix the soup well.

Fresh from a
Monastery Garden

Tomato and Mozzarella Salad

4 SERVINGS

4 red ripe tomatoes

2 yellow ripe tomatoes

1 red onion, thinly sliced and separated
    into rings

12 fresh basil leaves, (or more according
    to taste)

$^1/_2$ pound fresh mozzarella cheese, sliced

fruity olive oil to taste

balsamic vinegar to taste

salt and freshly ground pepper to taste

black olives as garnish (2 per plate)
    (optional)

1. Wash the tomatoes well. Slice them evenly. Distribute the slices evenly on four serving plates.

2. Add next to the tomato slices on each plate an equal amount of the onion rings, fresh basil leaves, and slices of mozzarella.

3. Just before serving, sprinkle lightly over each serving, the olive oil and vinegar to taste. Sprinkle also a bit of the salt and fresh black pepper to taste. Add 2 of the black olives to each plate as garnish.

Note: Use this dish to serve as an appetizer at lunch or supper.

Tomatoes

Tomatillo Green Sauce

(SALSA VERDE)

MAKES ABOUT 4 CUPS

1 pound tomatillos, sliced in halves or
    quarters

2 medium-size onions, chopped

3 garlic cloves

2 green bell peppers, seeded and chopped

1 small green chile pepper, fresh, canned,
    or pickled

1/2 cup fresh cilantro

1/2 cup plus 3 tablespoons olive oil

2 tablespoons lime juice

1 cup water

1 1/2 teaspoons salt

1. Combine all the ingredients except the 3 tablespoons olive oil in a blender jar or in a food processor and blend until it becomes a smooth sauce.

2. Pour the 3 tablespoons of the olive oil into a deep, heavy skillet or saucepan. Pour the tomatillo sauce into it and simmer over low heat while stirring continually for 10–15 minutes. Set the sauce aside and cool.

3. When the sauce is done, it can be used immediately, frozen for later use, or canned in small sterilized jars for future use.

Note: The Tomatillo Green Sauce is excellent accompanying Mexican or Southwestern dishes.

Tomatillo Dip

MAKES 2 CUPS

1. Prepare the Tomatillo Green Sauce as indicated above. Let it cool.

2. Mix 1 cup of the sauce with 1 cup of the sour cream. Blend thoroughly by hand. Place the dip in the refrigerator until you are ready to use it.

3. Serve the dip with tortillas or corn chips.

Tomatoes à la Joinville

6 tomatoes (medium size)

40 shrimp, well washed and thinly sliced

2 tablespoons lemon juice

1/2 cup mayonnaise of your preference or
   homemade

a pinch of cayenne pepper (optional)

12 pitted black olives as garnish

lettuce leaves

1. Wash the tomatoes well and carefully cut them at the middle into two even pieces. With the help of a thin knife and small spoon, scoop out the insides of the tomatoes with care. Place the insides of the tomatoes in a blender and whirl three or four times. Place the tomato puree in a large bowl.

2. Boil the sliced shrimp for exactly 5 minutes in salted lemony water (2 tablespoons lemon juice). Drain the shrimp and place them in the refrigerator for 1/2 hour until you are ready to use them.

3. Just before serving, add the shrimp, mayonnaise, and a pinch of cayenne pepper to the tomato puree and mix it all very well. (This should be refrigerated if it is not used immediately.)

4. Spread 2 or 3 lettuce leaves on each serving plate and place 2 tomato halves in the center of the plate. Fill each of them to the top with the shrimp mixture, place an olive in the center of each tomato, and serve soon after.

Note: This dish can be served as the main course for a light lunch during the summer months or as an appetizer for an attractive dinner.

Tomato Salad Alsatian Style

(TOMATES À L'ALSACIENNE)

6 tomatoes, washed and sliced into
　quarters

6 small potatoes, peeled, boiled, and sliced
　into quarters

1 good-size Bermuda onion, finely
　chopped

5 hard-boiled eggs, sliced into
　quarters

$^1/_2$ cup finely chopped fresh parsley

pitted green olives, sliced in halves, as
　garnish

VINAIGRETTE

7 tablespoons olive oil

3 tablespoons white vinegar

salt and freshly ground pepper to taste

1. Place the vegetables and the eggs in a deep bowl. Add the parsley. Mix together all the ingredients for the vinaigrette. Pour the dressing over the salad. Toss gently a few times before serving.

2. When ready to serve, distribute the salad evenly on six plates. Add a few sliced olives on top of each serving as garnish.

Note: This appetizing salad can be eaten as the main course for a brunch or lunch, or as an appetizer before the main course.

Tomatoes Stuffed with Goat Cheese

(TOMATES FARCIES AU CHÈVRE)

4 SERVINGS

4 medium-size ripe tomatoes

10 ounces goat cheese

4 tablespoons olive oil

a pinch of thyme

a pinch of rosemary

salt and pepper to taste

1. Preheat the oven to 300°. Slice off the tops of the tomatoes and then with great care hollow out their insides. Place them upside down over a paper towel to get rid of the remaining water (for at least 10–15 minutes).

2. In a deep bowl, mix the goat cheese, oil, thyme, rosemary, salt, and pepper. Mix all the ingredients well with the help of a fork. Divide this mixture into 4 equal portions, and place each portion inside the tomatoes.

3. Place the stuffed tomatoes into a well-buttered flat baking dish. Bake the tomatoes at 300° for about 20 minutes.

Note: This is a delicious dish to serve as an appetizer or even as a main course. If it is served as an appetizer, serve on top of leaves of lettuce as garnish. If it is served as a main course, add some plain white rice cooked with herbs on the side.

Tomatoes

Tomatoes Provençal Style

8 SERVINGS

8 medium-to-large firm tomatoes

8 tablespoons olive oil

1 onion, finely chopped

4 garlic cloves, minced

4 tablespoons finely chopped parsley

4 tablespoons finely chopped basil

1 teaspoon minced thyme

1 teaspoon rosemary, crumbled

1 egg

$^1/_3$ cup milk

1 cup bread crumbs

salt and pepper to taste

grated cheese, preferably Gruyère
(optional)

1. Wash and rinse the tomatoes. Cut off and discard the tops, just a little below the stem, and carefully scoop out the pulp with a small spoon.

2. Heat the oil in a large skillet, then add the tomato pulp, onion, garlic, and finely chopped and minced herbs. Sauté the mixture for a few minutes until it all blends well.

3. In a deep bowl, beat the egg with the milk, add the contents of the skillet, bread crumbs and salt and pepper to taste. Mix very well and fill the empty tomatoes with this mixture. You can sprinkle the tops of the tomatoes with grated cheese. Grease a flat baking dish and delicately place the tomatoes on it. Bake them at 350° for about 30 minutes. Serve them hot.

Turnips

(brassica napus)

The origin of the turnip is unknown, although traces remain that provide evidence that it was already in use during prehistoric times. Both the Romans and the Greeks held this humble root vegetable in high esteem. During the Middle Ages, the turnip, together with the cabbage, were probably the most popular vegetables in Europe. Once America was discovered, the turnip also began to appear in the New World under the influence of English, Spanish, and French colonists, who had a certain predilection for the turnip.

Today, there are several varieties of turnips available. They come in all types of sizes, colors, and shapes. Here in the monastic garden, we are provided with excellent seeds from France, and cultivate at least several varieties. First of all we cultivate a certain type of small white turnip, which is very tender and a great delicacy in many of our home dishes. Then there is the yellow turnip from France, which is wonderful in soup and pureed dishes. There is also the well-known white turnip with a bit of purple on the top, which is easy to grow and appears in most supermarkets. One type of turnip we don't grow in our garden and which is seldom used at the table is the rutabaga, which belongs to a different category of the turnip family.

Turnips contain a great deal of water and a certain amount of sugar. They also contain vitamins A and B. It is unfortunate that this humble vegetable is not taken more seriously, both by cooks and gardeners. In ancient times, the turnip was used as a remedy for many illnesses, especially those of pulmonary origin, for instance asthma and others. It was also said to be of salutary influence on the stomach. I think it is about time to rediscover the culinary value of the turnip and make more frequent use of it at the table.

269

Turnips

Turnips Country Style

8 firm medium-size white turnips

a pinch of salt

walnut oil, as needed

salt and pepper to taste

finely chopped chervil as garnish or (for non-vegetarians) finely chopped cooked bacon bits (optional)

1. Wash the turnips well and trim them at both ends. Cut them in 1-inch-thick round slices.

2. Place the turnip slices in a saucepan filled with water, add a pinch of salt, and bring the liquid to a quick boil. Boil the turnips for 1 minute and drain them immediately, pouring cold water over them. Set them aside and allow to dry.

3. Just before serving, heat the oil in a deep frying pan over medium-low heat and carefully add the turnip slices. Stir them carefully with the help of a spatula and allow them to brown on both sides. Add the seasonings as needed. Garnish with the chopped chervil (or the bacon bits, as preferred) and serve the turnips immediately.

Note: The turnips prepared this way are a good accompaniment to a main course and can take the place of the much used potato.

Turnips and Carrots in Maple Syrup

a pinch of salt

6 medium-size white turnips, washed and
    cubed

3 carrots, cubed

4 tablespoons butter

1 tablespoon dried mustard

1 tablespoon brown sugar

4 tablespoons maple syrup

a pinch of ginger

salt and freshly ground pepper to taste

1 1.5-ounce box dried raisins (optional)

1. Bring water to a boil in a good-size casserole and add a pinch of salt. Add the cubed turnips and carrots. Boil them for 6–7 minutes and drain them immediately. Set them aside.

2. Melt the butter in a large, deep skillet over medium-low heat. Add the mustard, sugar, maple syrup, and ginger, mixing it all together very well. Reduce the heat to low and add the turnips and carrots, salt and pepper to taste, and raisins. Stir the mixture often until all the cubes are well coated with the maple syrup sauce.

3. Preheat the oven to 300° and thoroughly butter a sufficiently deep ovenproof dish with a lid. Place the vegetables neatly in the dish, covering with the lid or aluminum foil. Bake the vegetables for 25–30 minutes. Serve them hot as an accompaniment to the main course.

Turnips au Gratin

(NAVETS AU GRATIN)

6 SERVINGS

2 pounds small white turnips
1 large Bermuda onion, chopped
3 garlic cloves, minced
6 tablespoons olive oil

2 teaspoons caraway seeds
salt and pepper to taste
$^1/_3$ cup grated cheese (Parmesan or other)

1. Wash and clean the turnips. Slice them and place them in a large casserole with salted water and bring the water to a boil. Reduce the heat to medium-low and continue cooking the turnips for 10 minutes until they are tender.

2. Preheat the oven to 350° and place the onion and garlic in a good-size frying pan. Pour in the oil and sauté lightly over low heat. Add the caraway seeds, salt and pepper, and cooked turnip slices. Cook for about 5 minutes and then set the pan aside for a few minutes. Add half of the cheese, mix all well, and then mash thoroughly with the help of a masher.

3. Thoroughly coat with olive oil (or use butter if preferred) an elongated ovenproof dish. Transfer the turnip mixture to the dish and sprinkle over the top the remaining grated cheese. Bake for 25–30 minutes. Serve hot as an accompaniment to the main course.

Note: These turnips go well with fish, meat, or egg dishes.

Fresh from a
Monastery Garden

Turnip Timbales
(TIMBALES DES NAVETS)

9 medium-size white turnips, peeled and
    cubed

2 tablespoons butter

3 eggs

1 8-ounce container half and half

salt and white pepper to taste

1/4 teaspoon nutmeg

finely chopped fresh chervil or fresh
    parsley as garnish

1. Bring water to a boil in a large casserole and add the cubed turnips. Cook them for 30 minutes. Drain them and then process the turnips in a food processor until they turn into a puree of even consistency.

2. Melt the butter in the casserole and add the pureed turnips. Continue cooking them over low heat for a few minutes stirring continually so the bottom does not burn. After cooking for 3 or 4 minutes, remove the casserole from the stove and let it cool.

3. Break the eggs into a blender, add the half and half and seasonings. Whirl in the blender and mix thoroughly. Gradually pour this mixture into the pureed turnips while whisking the mixture with the other hand. Mix well.

4. Heat the oven to 350° and butter thoroughly six small ramekins. Place the turnip mixture carefully and evenly into each ramekin.

5. Again, carefully put the ramekins into an elongated roasting pan and fill with water up to half the height of the ramekins. Bake the timbales for about 45 minutes or at least until they are firm and smooth. Add more water if necessary during the process so that the pan is never dry.

6. When the timbales are done, remove them carefully from the water bath and allow to cool for 1 minute before unmolding them from their ramekins. To unmold them, go around the edges of the timbales with a small thin knife. Do this slowly and with great care, then place a small plate on top of the ramekin and quickly turn it upside down. Lift the ramekin off with special care so the timbale remains intact. The timbale can be served hot or cold, garnished with the finely chopped chervil on top.

Turnips

Zucchini and Yellow Squash

(*cucurbita pepo*)

The zucchini and the yellow squash belong to the *cucurbita* family, as do all the squash. If they are treated differently here, it is because I consider them to be summertime vegetables. The rest of the squash can appropriately be called winter vegetables, since they are generally harvested at the end of the growing season when winter begins.

The zucchini squash seems to have originated in India where it has been cultivated for many centuries. The zucchini and the yellow squash, as with the other types of squash, cultivate well in warm-weather climates. This is one reason why we never plant it here in our gardens before the beginning of May. Sometimes, if spring remains cooler than usual, we will even wait until after the middle of May to sow the first seeds. In the monastery garden, we usually grow three different types of this form of squash: the so-called yellow squash, the Cocozella zucchini, *coucourzelle* in French, and the Ronde de Nice, which is a round-variety type of zucchini, cultivated throughout Provence in France, from where we import the seeds. This last type of squash we usually serve at the table in a baked form. It usually has more taste than the other zucchini, and when stuffed with day-old bread and Provençal herbs it becomes a true culinary delight.

The zucchini has achieved great popularity in Italy and France as well as throughout the United States. One of its qualities is its versatility, for it lends itself to many uses, from the popular zucchini bread to baked zucchini and zucchini soups. It harmonizes well with other vegetables and other ingredients, and it demands very little time for cooking, which makes it an ideal vegetable to prepare when one is pressed for time.

Zucchini and
Yellow Squash

Zucchini Monegasque Style
(COURGETTES À LA MONÉGASQUE)

4–6 SERVINGS

6 tender medium-size zucchini

6 tomatoes, boiled, peeled, and sliced

1 onion, sliced

10 basil leaves, chopped

8 tablespoons olive oil

salt and pepper to taste

1 cup grated cheese

1. Slice the zucchini evenly in thin pieces.

2. Sauté the tomatoes, onion, and basil in 3 tablespoons of the olive oil until the mixture becomes a good tasty sauce. Season it with salt and pepper. When the sauce is done, remove it from the heat.

3. Grease an ovenproof baking dish with butter or olive oil. Place in layers the zucchini, grated cheese, and tomato sauce. Repeat the layers once more and cover the top with the remaining olive oil.

4. Place the baking dish in a 300° preheated oven for 25 or 30 minutes. Serve hot as an accompaniment to a main dish.

Note: Yellow squash can be substituted for the zucchini in this dish.

Fresh from a
Monastery Garden

Basic Zucchini Velouté

(VELOUTÉ DE COURGETTES)

4 SERVINGS

2 zucchini

2 leeks

3 tablespoons olive oil

6 cups water

a few mint leaves, chopped, for both the
velouté and as garnish

salt and freshly ground pepper to taste

1 8-ounce container low-fat sour cream or
yogurt

1. Wash and clean the zucchini well. Cut into thick slices. Wash and clean the leeks well. Slice the white parts of the leeks and discard the green tops.

2. Pour the oil into a soup pot. Add the zucchini and leeks and sauté over medium-low heat for about 3 minutes. Stir frequently.

3. Add the water, mint leaves, and salt and pepper. Stir well. Cover the soup pot, bring the water to a boil, and then lower the heat to medium-low. Keep the pan covered and let the soup cook gently for about 20–25 minutes. Set the soup aside and allow it to cool.

4. Once the soup has cooled, add the sour cream or yogurt. Mix the soup well and then blend it in small batches in a blender. Blend for several minutes until it reaches a fine even consistency. Place the soup in the refrigerator for at least 2 hours. Serve cold, adding the finely chopped mint leaves on top of each serving as garnish.

Zucchini and
Yellow Squash

Quick Yellow Squash and Pasta Dish

4 SERVINGS

3 medium-size new yellow squash, sliced (not too thin)

2 cups rotini pasta (or any other of your preference)

2 tablespoons plus $^{1}/_{3}$ cup good olive oil

salt to taste

$^{3}/_{4}$ cup chopped fresh basil leaves

4 garlic cloves, peeled

freshly ground pepper to taste

1 cup cherry tomatoes

grated Parmesan cheese for the table

1. Pour a sufficient amount of water into a large casserole and bring it to a boil. Add the sliced squash, pasta, 2 tablespoons of the olive oil, and salt, and cook for about 8–10 minutes over medium heat. Stir occasionally and don't overcook. The pasta must remain al dente.

2. While the squash and pasta are cooking, prepare the basil-garlic sauce by placing them in a food processor and adding the remaining $^{1}/_{3}$ cup of olive oil and some freshly ground pepper. Whirl for 1 minute until the sauce acquires a smooth consistency.

3. Slice the cherry tomatoes into halves and set them aside.

4. When the squash and pasta are cooked, drain them and place them back in the casserole. Add the basil sauce and sliced cherry tomatoes, and mix this with care. Serve immediately after accompanied by grated cheese at the table.

Note: This is an excellent dish to serve as a main course during the summer months when the fresh vegetables are available from the garden.

Fresh from a
Monastery Garden

Zucchini Compote with Coriander

(COMPOTE DE COURGETTES À LA CORIANDRE)

4 SERVINGS

8 small tender zucchini

2 onions

6 tablespoons olive oil

juice of 1 lemon

15 coriander seeds

1 cup water

salt and pepper to taste

finely chopped fresh mint leaves as
 garnish

1. Slice the zucchini (not too thin) and chop and mince the onions.

2. Pour the olive oil into a fairly deep skillet. Add the zucchini, onions, juice from the lemon, coriander seeds, water, and salt and pepper. Cover the pot and cook over medium-low heat for about 15–20 minutes. Check after 15 minutes to make sure the vegetables don't overcook. Stir gently.

3. Garnish the compote with the finely chopped mint leaves. Serve the zucchini compote warm or cold as an accompaniment to eggs, fish, meat, beans, lentils, rice, etc.

Zucchini and
Yellow Squash

Yellow and Zucchini Squash with Wine

6–8 SERVINGS

3 yellow squash, chopped in sticks as for french fries

3 zucchini, chopped as above

6 tablespoons olive oil

2 medium-size onions, sliced

I cup dry white wine (more if necessary)

2 garlic cloves, minced

2 tablespoons lemon juice

chopped fresh basil leaves, to taste

chopped fresh parsley, to taste

salt and pepper to taste

grated Parmesan cheese as garnish

1. If the squash and zucchini are too large be sure to discard the seeds.

2. Pour the olive oil into a deep, large skillet, add the onions, and sauté them over medium-low heat for about 2 minutes. Stir continuously. Add the yellow and zucchini squash and continue sautéing for another 2 minutes while stirring along. Add the wine, mix and toss gently. Cover the skillet, reduce the heat to low, and cook thus for 5–6 minutes until the wine begins to evaporate.

3. At this point, add the minced garlic, lemon juice, herbs, salt, and pepper. Toss gently for a few seconds until all the ingredients are well mixed and then remove the skillet from the heat. Serve the squash hot, and sprinkle grated Parmesan cheese on top.

Note: This accompanies grain dishes such as rice, millet, couscous, lentils, etc., well. It also goes well with fish and poultry dishes.

Fresh from a
Monastery Garden

Stuffed Ronde de Nice Zucchini

6 SERVINGS

3 Ronde de Nice zucchini

3 tablespoons olive oil

2 medium onions, chopped

2 garlic cloves, minced

1 tablespoon chopped sage

1 tablespoon thyme

a few fresh parsley sprigs, chopped

3 or 4 slices of brown bread, crumbled, as needed

2 eggs

½ cup milk

salt and pepper to taste

grated Parmesan or Gruyère cheese as topping

1. Slice the round zucchini in perfect halves. Scoop out the seeds. Leave the rest intact. Place the shells upside down in salted boiling water and boil them for about 3 minutes. Drain them carefully and set them aside.

2. Pour the oil into a frying pan, add the onions and all the herbs, including the fresh parsley, and sauté them over medium-low heat for about 3 minutes until the onions begin to turn brown. Add the crumbled bread and mix all the ingredients well. Turn off the heat and set the pan aside.

3. Beat the eggs in a deep bowl. Add the milk and salt and pepper and beat some more until they are well mixed. Add the onion-bread mixture and mix some more.

4. Thoroughly butter a long Pyrex or other ovenproof dish and carefully place the zucchini shells into it. Fill each one to the top with the onion-egg mixture. Cover each top with grated cheese. Place the dish in a 300° preheated oven and bake for 30 minutes. Serve hot.

Zucchini and
Yellow Squash

Preservation and Canning of Vegetables (and select recipes)

CANNING STEPS

Canning of fruits or vegetables follows these steps.

1. Preparation: Ensure that the rims of the glass jars are not cracked or chipped. The metal lids must have a complete ring of sealant, and ideally each lid is used only once and then discarded.

2. Sterilization: Jars and tops must be cleaned by being placed in boiling water for 20 minutes. The water should be boiled, then removed from the heat, prior to immersion of the material.

3. Filling: After the water is removed and the jars are dried, place the vegetables in the jar, loosely packed. For vegetables, fill the jars up to 1 inch from the top with the vegetable and with the liquid in which the vegetable was boiled.

4. Sealing: Poke a nonmetallic utensil down into the materials to dislodge air bubbles. Clean the jar rim and top, and cover with a lid. Screw on the sealing band, ensuring that the band fits tightly.

5. Processing: Use a pressure canner to complete the sterilization of the canned vegetables. Follow the instructions of your pressure canner to ensure properly processed food. Following this step, allow the canned food to cool.

Some food products do not need a pressure canner: tomatoes, pickles, jellies, and sauces. These can be boiled in a large pot with the canned vegetables completely immersed in water. Prior to placing the jars in the water, make sure you put a rack on the bottom of the pot to avoid allowing the glass containers to touch the bottom of the pot. Do not over pack the pot with jars; allow enough room for water to circulate between the jars. Boil for 30–40 minutes for sauces, 80 minutes for whole vegetables (tomatoes).

6. Verification: Once the jars have been sterilized, test for a proper seal—the lid should be slightly curved inward. If the seal has not been made, the jar can be tightened and the sterilization process repeated.

Note: It is important that sterilization and processing are done for an adequate length of time to ensure that all microorganisms are killed, and that a proper seal is achieved.

Preservation and
Canning of Vegetables

Yellow Squash–Zucchini Relish

MAKES ABOUT 2 PINTS

2 cups chopped squash and zucchini

1 onion, chopped

1 green bell pepper, chopped

1 red bell pepper, chopped

2 tablespoons salt

$1^3/_4$ cups sugar

1 cup cider vinegar

2 teaspoons celery seed

1 teaspoon mustard seed

1. Combine the zucchini and squash, onion, and green and red peppers. Shake the salt over all and cover with cold water. Let stand for 2 hours and then drain out the water, pressing the vegetables to remove as much moisture as possible.

2. In another pot, combine the rest of the ingredients and bring them to a boil. Add the vegetables and simmer for 10 minutes.

3. Pack the hot mixture into the hot jars, up to $^1/_4$ inch from the top. Cover the jars and seal them by placing them in boiling water, covering the jars completely. Boil them for at least 15 minutes. Remove the jars from the water bath and allow them to cool. Make sure the tops are thoroughly sealed.

Basic Monastery Salsa

MAKES ABOUT 6 PINTS

10 cups peeled, cored, and chopped
tomatoes

5 bell peppers, chopped

5 cups chopped onions

1 jalapeño pepper, cored, seeded, and
chopped

1 1/4 cups cider vinegar

4 cloves garlic, minced

4 tablespoons minced cilantro

3 tablespoons minced fresh parsley

3 teaspoons salt

1/2 teaspoon hot pepper

1. Place all the ingredients in a large saucepan. Bring the mixture to a boil and simmer for 20 minutes.

2. Pack the hot mixture into hot jars, up to 1/4 inch from the top. Cover the jars and seal them by placing them in boiling water, covering the jars completely. Boil them for at least 15 minutes. Remove the jars from the water bath and allow them to cool before placing them in storage. Make sure the tops are thoroughly sealed.

289

Preservation and
Canning of Vegetables

Basic Tomato Sauce

MAKES ABOUT 7 PINTS

1 large onion, diced

3 garlic cloves, minced

2 tablespoons olive oil

20 tomatoes, peeled, cored, and chopped

1 green bell pepper, diced

1 tablespoon chopped oregano

10 tablespoons chopped basil leaves

1 tablespoon chopped rosemary

1 teaspoon salt

$^{1}/_{2}$ teaspoon pepper

1. Cook the diced onion and minced garlic in the oil in a large saucepan until tender. Add all the remaining ingredients and bring to a boil; reduce the heat to low, simmering for 1 hour and stirring occasionally.

2. Process the mixture in a food processor. Cook the mixture over medium-low heat for 1 hour, until the mixture thickens. Stir to prevent sticking.

3. Pour the mixture into hot jars, up to $^{1}/_{4}$ inch from the top. Cover the jars and seal them by placing them in boiling water, covering the jars completely. Boil them for at least 30 minutes. Remove the jars from the water bath and allow them to cool. Make sure the tops are thoroughly sealed.

Fresh from a
Monastery Garden

Monastery Corn Relish

18 ears of corn

3 medium zucchini, diced

1 large onion, diced

2 green bell peppers, chopped

2 red bell peppers, chopped

1 cup sugar

2 tablespoons dry mustard

1 tablespoon mustard seed

1 tablespoon turmeric

1 tablespoon celery seed

1 tablespoon salt

1 quart vinegar (white)

1 cup water

1. Prepare the corn: place the corn for 5 minutes in boiling water and then cut the corn from the cob. Place all the ingredients along with the corn in a large saucepan. Bring the mixture to a boil and simmer for 20 minutes.

2. Pack the hot mixture into hot jars, up to $^1/_2$ inch from the top. Cover the jars and seal them by processing them in boiling water. Make sure that the jars are completely immersed in water. After boiling them for 15 minutes, remove the jars and allow them to cool. Make sure the tops are thoroughly sealed.

Preservation and
Canning of Vegetables

Provençal Tomato Sauce

20 tomatoes, peeled, cored, and chopped

2 celery stalks, sliced

2 carrots, sliced

1 large onion, chopped

3 garlic cloves, minced

12 basil leaves

1 bay leaf

salt and pepper to taste

Combine all ingredients in a large saucepot. Cover and cook 30 minutes, stirring to prevent sticking. Pour into hot jars, up to 1 inch from the top. Cover the jars and seal them by placing them in a boiling water bath, with water covering the tops of the jars. Boil them for at least 30 minutes, then remove the jars from the water and allow them to cool. Make sure the tops are thoroughly sealed.

Fresh from a
Monastery Garden

Tuscan Tomato Sauce

MAKES ABOUT 7 PINTS

20 tomatoes, peeled, cored, and chopped

1 celery stalk, sliced

2 zucchini, diced

1 large onion, chopped

1 8-ounce can pitted black olives, drained

6 garlic cloves, minced

1 green bell pepper, chopped

2 tablespoons sugar

4 tablespoons olive oil

10 basil leaves

1 bay leaf

salt and pepper to taste

Combine all the ingredients in a large saucepot. Cover the pot and cook 30 minutes, stirring to prevent sticking. Pour the sauce into hot jars, up to $1/2$ inch from the top. Cover the jars and seal them by placing them in a boiling water bath, covering the tops of the jars. Boil them for 30 minutes, then remove the jars and allow them to cool. Make sure the tops are thoroughly sealed.

Cucumber Relish

8 cucumbers, diced

5 green bell peppers, finely chopped

3 red bell peppers, finely chopped

4 cloves garlic, minced

1 onion, finely chopped

1 tablespoon turmeric

$^1/_2$ cup salt

2 quarts cold water

1$^1/_2$ cups brown sugar

1 quart white vinegar

1 tablespoon mustard seed

2 teaspoons whole allspice

2 teaspoons whole cloves

1. Combine the cucumbers, peppers, garlic, and onion in a large pot. Shake the turmeric over all. In another pot, dissolve the salt in 2 quarts of cold water, and pour the water over the vegetables. Let this stand for 3–4 hours. Drain the water, cover the vegetables with cold water, and let stand 1 hour. Drain the water.

2. Combine the sugar and vinegar in a saucepan. Tie the spices in a cheesecloth bag and add it to the pan. Bring the mixture to a boil, and pour it over the vegetables. Cover the pot and let the vegetables stand for 10 hours in a cool place.

3. Bring the vegetables to a boil. Simmer until they are hot. Pack the hot vegetables into the hot jars, up to $^1/_4$ inch from top. Cover the jars and place them in a large pot, covering them with boiling water, and boil them for at least 20 minutes. Remove the jars from the water bath and allow them to cool. Make sure the tops are thoroughly sealed.

Fresh from a
Monastery Garden

Salty Cucumber Pickles

MAKES ABOUT 3 PINTS

1/3 cup canning salt

2 pounds cucumbers, cut into 1/4-inch-
thick slices

2 quarts cold water

4 cups water

5 cups white vinegar

1 cup brown sugar

1 teaspoon celery seed

1 teaspoon mustard seed

1. Pour the salt lightly over the cut cucumbers; add the 2 quarts of cold water to the cucumbers and let them stand for 2 1/2 hours. Drain off all the water.

2. In a separate pot, boil 3 cups of the water and 3 cups of the vinegar together. Add the cucumbers to this mixture and allow them to simmer for 8 minutes. Remove the cucumbers and set aside, discarding the mixture.

3. Create a new mixture of the remaining 1 cup of water and the remaining 2 cups vinegar. Add the brown sugar and celery and mustard seeds and bring this to a boil. Simmer for 10 minutes. Add the cucumbers. Bring the mixture to a boil. Fill jars with the mixture up to 1/2 inch from the top. Cover the jars and seal them by placing them in a large pot, covering them with boiling water, and boiling them for at least 20 minutes. Remove the jars from the water bath and allow them to cool. Ensure that a tight seal has been formed.

Preservation and
Canning of Vegetables

Peach-Zucchini Chutney

MAKES ABOUT 8 PINTS

20 peaches, peeled and chopped

2 medium-size zucchini, diced

³/4 cup raisins

1 large onion, chopped

2 cups brown sugar

1 tablespoon cumin

2 tablespoons ginger

¹/4 cup mustard seed

2 teaspoons salt

2 cloves garlic, minced

1 red pepper, minced

5 cups vinegar

Place all the ingredients in a large saucepan. Simmer until thick, about 40 minutes. As the mixture becomes thick, stir often to avoid sticking. Pour the chutney into hot jars, up to ¹/4 inch from the top. Cover the jars and seal them by placing them in boiling water (covering the jar over the tops), and boiling them for at least 20 minutes. Remove the jars from the water bath and allow them to cool. Make sure the tops are thoroughly sealed.

Apple–Sweet Potato Chutney

12 tart apples, peeled and chopped

4 sweet potatoes, peeled, chopped, cooked,
  and mashed

2 onions, chopped

2 red peppers, diced

2½ cups brown sugar

2 teaspoons cumin

2 teaspoons allspice

3 tablespoons mustard seed

2 tablespoons ginger

2 hot red peppers, chopped

2 teaspoons salt

3 cloves garlic, minced

1 quart cider vinegar

Place all the ingredients in a large saucepan. Simmer until thick, about 1 hour. As the mixture becomes thick, stir often to avoid sticking. Pour the mixture into hot jars, up to ¼ inch from the top. Cover the jars and seal them by placing them in boiling water (covering the tops of the jars), and boiling them for at least 20 minutes. Make sure the tops are thoroughly sealed.

Note: This can be made as hot (spicy) as you desire by increasing the sources of spiciness (hot peppers, mustard, ginger). Alternatively, the dish can be made milder by removing the seeds from the hot pepper, which are a major source of the hot sting.

SOME TIPS ON CHOOSING AND
PREPARING VEGETABLES

1. Always choose fresh vegetables and fruits, whether from your own garden, a farmer's roadside stand, or the supermarket. Fresh produce preserves the vital vitamins, nutrients, and fiber needed for your health.

2. Try to obtain and experiment with the vegetables that are currently in season. Use what is most available, which tends to assure the freshness of the produce. The changing variety of produce throughout the year also seems to suit the varying needs of our bodies. Besides, vegetables that are in season also tend to be more economical.

3. When you purchase your vegetables, avoid those that look old, damaged, or somehow tarnished. The younger, the fresher, the firmer the produce, the more it preserves its original taste, texture, and nutritional value.

4. Whenever possible, ascertain that the vegetables you use are grown organically, free of pesticides. If possible, cultivate your own vegetables in order to avoid any chemical substances such as pesticides that can be dangerous to your health. When you are not sure of the provenance of the vegetables, wash and clean them thoroughly.

5. It is important to prepare and preserve your vegetables properly. Use the refrigerator for those vegetables that need the colder temperatures. Some vegetables and fruits such as potatoes, squash, apples, etc., can be kept adequately in a cool, dry cellar.

6. If the vegetables that you use in the kitchen are from your garden or are organically grown, you can use the entire vegetable, including the outer covering. The peel often contains important vitamins and nutrients. However, if you are doubtful about how they have been grown, it may be safer to peel them or scrub them under running water.

7. Some vegetables such as celery root, artichokes, avocados, etc., tend to oxidize and change color. Use lemon or white vinegar to preserve them from any oxidation and to conserve their original color.

8. When cooking vegetables, do not overcook. Overcooking tends to diminish the nutritional content as well as the taste and texture or the original vegetable. Learn to use the techniques appropriate for each particular vegetable.

Fresh from a
Monastery Garden

9. Always save the water in which your vegetables are cooked or boiled. Refrigerate and use it as vegetable bouillon in your next soup. This contains good nutrition, and it is delicious as well.

10. The right presentation of vegetables at the table is important. It must be attractive and appealing visually, as well as for the taste and aroma. Besides their nutritional value, vegetables for soups or other dishes should be chosen on the basis of flavor, shape, color, and texture for as healthy and appetizing a diet as possible.

11. When using leafy vegetables that are not from your own garden or from a garden following natural organic methods—vegetables such as lettuce, cabbage, and others—remove their outer leaves, trimming areas that may contain residues of pesticides and chemicals that have collected there.

VEGETABLES RECOMMENDED FOR USE IN ACCORDANCE WITH THE SEASONS

SPRING

Asparagus	Jerusalem artichokes	Radishes
Avocados	Salad greens	Spinach
Beets	Mushrooms	Sorrel
Carrots	Onions	Lentils
Endive	Sweet peas	Chick peas
Grains and cereals	Potatoes	Split peas

SUMMER

Artichokes	Celery	Onions
Beans	Corn	Peppers
Beets	Cucumber	Potatoes
Broccoli	Egg Plant	Radishes
Cauliflower	Cereals and grains	Tomatoes
Carrots	Salad greens	Zucchini
Celery root	Okra	Summer squash (yellow)

Vegetables and Their Seasons

AUTUMN

Artichokes	Salad greens	Tomatoes
Beans	Swiss chard	Turnips
Cabbage	Spinach	Zucchini
Carrots	Leeks	Watercress
Broccoli	Mushrooms	Radicchio
Cauliflower	Onions	Brussels sprouts
Corn	Sweet peas	Mâche
Cucumber	Peppers	Sorrel
Eggplant	Potatoes	Pumpkin
Fennel	Squash	Sweet potatoes
Grains and cereals	Radishes	

WINTER

Avocados	Jerusalem artichokes	Brussels sprouts
Beets	Salad greens	Turnips
Cabbage	Leeks	Lentils
Carrots	Mushrooms	Dried beans
Celery root	Onions	Sweet potatoes
Celery	Potatoes	
Endive	Squash	

Fresh from a
Monastery Garden

INDEX

303

Index

Index

305

Index